Gary Lee is one of America's leading authorities on Wok cooking and oriental cuisine.

As a child, Mr. Lee was deeply influenced by China's ageless culture and traditions. These influences inspired him into the realm of cooking at an early age and in 1946 he left China and traveled to 100 ports as a Catering Officer on a foreign merchant ship. He then opened a gourmet Chinese restaurant in Brazil which he owned and operated for 16 years, specializing in authentic Chinese cuisine. During his career, Mr. Lee's cooking has been enjoyed by the President of Brazil, the Emperor of Japan and other foreign dignitaries.

In 1969, Gary moved to San Francisco and published his first cookbook, The Wok, which is known as one of the most complete cookbooks in the Chinese cooking field. He is now active as a professional chef and cooking teacher and was awarded the blue ribbon for Chinese Light Snacks at San Francisco's First Annual Food Exposition in June, 1982.

AUTHENTIC CHINESE APPETIZERS AND LIGHT SNACKS ARE **EASY** WITH THIS NEW COOKBOOK BY GARY LEE.

- Gary Lee is a master of Chinese cooking and author of THE WOK, the original, complete guide to oriental cooking.

- Contains delicious recipes for everything from egg rolls and won ton to shrimp, spareribs and steamed snacks—each with that authentic Gary Lee touch.

- Complete with entertaining ideas, cooking tips, and suggestions that will make any get-together special.

- As with all Nitty Gritty Cookbooks, the recipes are easy to follow and are printed one per page, in large, easy-to-read type.

- For added convenience, this book is uniquely designed to take a minimum of counter space and to keep your place when pressed open.

SATISFACTION GUARANTEE — If you are not completely satisfied with any Nitty Gritty book, we will gladly refund your purchase price. Simply return it to us within 30 days along with your receipt.

WOK Appetizers and Light Snacks

by Gary Lee

photographs by Glen Millward
illustrations by Mike Nelson
edited by Jackie Walsh

Dedication

No book is a one-man job. I owe many persons for their encouragement, inspiration, assistance and helping hands:

To Sir James Murray who gave me the opportunity to try Chinese recipes and diplomatically commented on the bad ones, inspiring me to improve my culinary skills.

To Herb Caen whose column inspired such recipes as Fish Ping Pong!

To students and staff of Delta College in sunny Stockton, California, I remember those friendly faces which kept me testing and teaching Chinese cuisine.

To editor, Jackie Walsh who expertly translated my recipes to a form that is easy to follow.

To Mike Nelson's art work and Glen Millward's photography—just beautiful!

To Hedy, my personal critic since we married in 1945, who has tirelessly rated my recipes with a system of nodding—oftentimes horizontally. Now this book is done with her nodding—vertically!

TABLE OF CONTENTS

INTRODUCTION

Appetizers, as the dictionary defines them, are small quantities of food eaten before a meal to stimulate the appetite. At many cocktail parties and receptions, appetizers are served exclusively with no meal to follow. In this case, there should be more of them and they can be of a richer variety. (See page 14 for more information on planning party appetizers.) If dinner is to follow, the appetizers should be light and simply tease the appetite, not satisfy it.

I have had years of experience preparing many kinds of appetizers for diplomatic parties and always I have adhered to Chinese culinary traditions. The appetizers I make must be small enough to be eaten with one's fingers, elegant in appearance and, of course, delicious.

Unlike appetizers, light snacks can be served almost anytime—breakfast, lunch, late evening or in between. According to Chinese tradition, the only time they cannot be served is in place of the evening meal. They can be warm or cold, sweet or savory. They, too, should be small and served in small quantities. As their name implies, they are light snacks.

Appetizers are served for special occasions to which friends and acquanitances have been invited. Light snacks, however, are more likely offered to close friends or family members after a game of bridge or Mah Jong.

Many of the appetizers in this cookbook may be served as light snacks, if desired. But, most of the light snacks would fail to qualify as appetizers. We cannot, for example, serve Mountainous Noodles as an appetizer.

Toasting Chinese Style

*In composing short verses in Portuguese, the Romance language of Brazil where I lived for 17 years, we can always control the ending adjective with an **a** or **o** like lind**a** or lind**o**, meaning pretty.*

In Chinese, rhymes are more difficult. There are too many rules to be followed—exact number of words, rigid rhythms, no direct approaches and subtleness that is hard to reach at the right degree.

English, too, is troublesome. There are far too many articles and prepositions and I do not have sufficient vocabulary to match the sounds. The following are some toasts, Chinese style, rewritten into English. You might enjoy them.

"Let us drink to our friendship in the past, present and neverending future!"

"Let us drink to the full moon, and to a mutual business boom!"

"Let us drink to the Amazon, which is always green; and that your name will always be seen!"

"Let us drink to the person who is bright and who is always doing right!"

"Let us drink to the evening, which is still young and to the person who is progressing!"

"The evening is no longer young (yawn); let us drink 'til dawn!"

HOW TO PLAN YOUR APPETIZERS

Planning appetizers for one or two, or up to five or six is not a problem. You usually know each person's favorite foods and can plan accordingly. Four or five different varieties can be easily managed. Because you need fewer total appetizers, fancy ones can be considered.

When the number of guests increases, planning the appetizers may seem more complicated. It really isn't when you have a guide to follow. I hope my suggestions and accompanying chart will be helpful. The amounts are figured for guests with average appetites. If teenagers are the majority, then the amounts must be doubled—or tripled! If a meal is to follow, the number per person should be smaller.

For ten people, five varieties of appetizers are recommended and you may have time to prepare a few fancy ones. For each additional ten people, add one more variety. Up to twelve varieties (for a gathering of eighty people) would be manageable by one person—you!

Allow five to six appetizers per person for smaller groups, depending whether light or heavy and how time consuming they are to make, and three to five for larger groups. Multiply the number of appetizers per person by the number of guests to determine the total number of appetizers needed. Then divide that number by the number of varieties you are planning. That will tell you how many of each variety will be needed for a specific size group. Use my chart to help you plan the number of appetizers you will need.

APPETIZER PLANNING CHART

Number of People	X	Number of Appetizers Per Person	=	Total Appetizers Needed	÷	Number of Varieties Recommended	=	Number of Each Variety to be Prepared
1 to 4		4 to 5		6 to 20		2 to 3		3 to 7
5 to 9		5 to 6		25 to 50		4		6 to 10
10		5 to 6		50 to 60		5		10 to 12
20		5 to 6		100 to 120		6		16 to 20
30		5 to 6		150 to 180		7		22 to 25
40		5		200		8		25
50		5		250		9		27

Unless you have helping hands don't try to prepare too many fancy appetizers for a large group. In that case you must use more open-faced sandwiches of various shapes and fillings to fullfill requirements.

Make your appetizers small, attractive and above all, delicious! Remember when they are fully consumed, you should be proud of your job. Too many left over—not a compliment!

GLOSSARY AND BASIC INFORMATION

BINDING MIXTURE—a simple paste used in many recipes. To prepare it, combine one tablespoon of cornstarch and an egg white.

BREAD
Dry breadcrumbs—should be unseasoned and fine in texture.
Fresh breadcrumbs—remove crusts from white bread. Place pieces of bread in blender or food processor. Blend or process until bread is crumb size.
To Dry Bread—place fresh white bread on rack at room temperature for an hour. To shorten process, dry in 150°F. oven for 10 to 15 minutes.

CHOPSTICKS—these are your extra, heat-resistant fingers. Learn how to use them. They are extremely helpful when deep-frying.

CILANTRO—also known as fresh coriander and Chinese parsley, was actually brought to China by the Portuguese hundreds of years ago. Its distinctive flavor was so pleasant to the Chinese that it has been used ever since.

Cilantro is popular in Latin American cuisine too. Only in the United States is cilantro referred to as Chinese parsley—an unjustified, though flattering honor to the Chinese!

Ordinary parsley is rarely used in Chinese cuisine, because it lacks flavor. It is true that parsley looks pretty for garnishing, retains its color and form longer at room temperature and, most importantly, is less expensive. For these reasons, parsley is used in many Chinese restaurants for garnishing only. When they want to garnish and add flavor, they always use cilantro.

One advantage of using cilantro to garnish foods is that it can be pasted atop food and will hold its natural shape—even after steaming or deep-frying. This is because it is flat, rather than curly, like ordinary parsley.

CROSS-CUT—is a cutting technique used for broccoli and cauliflower. Cut a cross through the stem, about an inch deep, so that the stem will form a four-pointed root. See broccoli in cover photograph.

DEEP-FRYING—When deep-frying, it is best always to use a thermometer. The oil should be at least two inches deep in a wok. Each batch cooked should be in an amount small enough to prevent the temerpature of the oil dropping more than 75°F. However, too small an amount will cause the food to burn and the inside will still be raw.

FIVE SPICE POWDER—A blend of star anise, cinnamon, cloves, fennel and pepper.

OIL

Buying in quantity—purchasing oil in a can or large plastic container is cheaper and saves you trips to the market. When you think there is no more oil in the can, make a tiny hole in the corner opposite the pouring hole. Prop the can over a bowl, against a corner of the counter wall. Leave the can upside down to drain. You will be surprised. At least one-quarter cup of oil will be in the bowl! Why should we waste it?

Peanut oil—is the preferred oil to use in deep-frying of Chinese foods.

Reusing oil—it's fine to re-use oil, but do it in a logical sequence. You may fry chicken, then meatballs, then shrimp, then fish, in the same oil. Never reverse the sequence. Oil that has been used to fry shrimp or fish cannot be used to fry

Continued

Oil continued

chicken or meatballs. To keep track of what the oil has been used for, it's a good idea to label it.

Storing oil—after frying, add one tablespoon of cornstarch per quart of oil. Let stand until cool. Sediments will settle to the bottom. Strain the oil and keep it in a cool, dark place.

Temperature—the maximum temperature recommended for home cooking is 350°F.

Sesame oil—always use Chinese sesame oil. Most American brands of sesame oil are refined and have no flavor.

PEPPER

Flower pepper—is fragrant and does not have a hot taste. Buy a package when you visit cities that have a Chinatown. Nutmeg may be substituted.

White pepper—is used a great deal in Chinese cooking because it produces a clean-looking product.

REHEATING FOOD—should be done in the oven with the door partially ajar. The fac-

tory installed latch that allows you to do this is too wide. Jam your oven with a piece of wood, or some other heat resistant material, so that the opening is only about one inch wide.

SHRIMP—should always be deveined, washed and dried with paper towels. According to the particular recipe, remove the tail or leave it intact.

SOY SAUCE—there are many different kinds of soy sauce. Use the light variety, if possible, because it is better for frying. Dark soy sauce often burns.

SUGAR—is used to balance the salt in a recipe, or to brown the food while it frys.

THE THREE MUSKETEERS—refers to the three essential pieces of equipment for Chinese cooking.

Chopping board—the type the Chinese use is a cross-section of pine. The soft wood offers little resistance to the sharp cleaver, allowing the cleaver to remain sharp. Another advantage of this type of wood is that it is coarse and therefore prevents the slippery motion that results from cutting on a board made from hard wood.

Cleaver—it is easy to keep a cleaver sharp. And, it's broad, square shape is perfect to pick up food with. You actually have a knife with a built-in scraper always on hand.

Wok—this is indispensable for Chinese cooking. It's the best utensil for deep- frying. Together with the above mentioned items and chopsticks, you can venture successfully into Chinese cuisine, just like D'Artagnan and the Three Musketeers did in Alexander Dumas' exciting novel.

VINEGAR— Always use malt vinegar. It is too difficult to find Chinese varieties.

WINE— when this is called for, it is best to use Chinese yellow rice wine. If making a substitution, remember, it must be dry. Dry vermouth is a good, inexpensive substitute.

A Moment To Chat with My Readers

In order to follow the format of this book as requested by Nitty Gritty, I could not afford to use a wasteful line, even lengthy words were replaced by shorter ones.

Because of the limited number of lines and spaces, I had to write and rewrite ten times to come up with a finished page where the details are retained, yet the text readable. I frankly liked the task. It's very neat and pleasant to the eye. I'm proud of the results and think this book will be greatly enjoyed by those who use it.

My recipes have been tried by many and have always won praise. I have high standards and take great pleasure in cooking for my family and guests. It makes me happy to know the appetizers and snacks you lovingly prepare from this collection of favorites will be enjoyed by your family and friends. Two things to remember: keep the servings small and make everything, no matter how simple, look attractive and appetizing.

If you have any comments or suggestions, I will be happy to hear from you. Please write me in care of Nitty Gritty. The address can be found on the inside back cover of this book.

I wish you good luck with my Chinese recipes. During this coffee break, may I have a cup of tea?

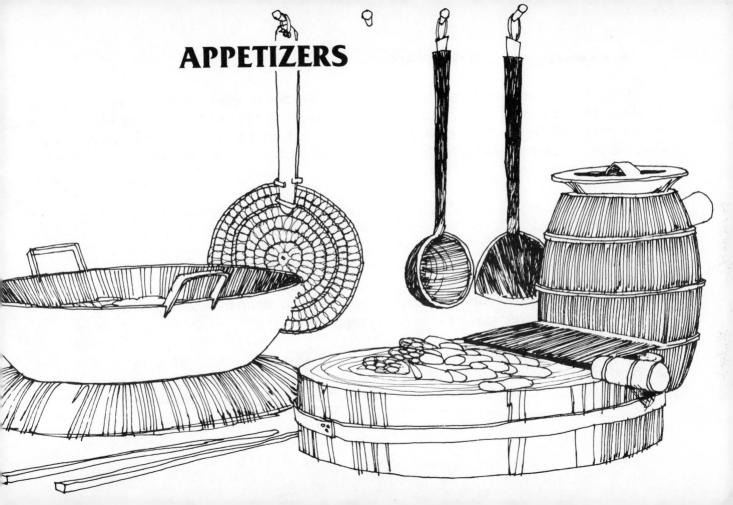

APPETIZERS

SHANGHAI MEATBALLS

The tenderness of meat can be improved by mixing in a proper choice of vegetables. So those who claim, "Our hamburgers are pure beef, no fillers!" are misleading you because the cost of adding vegetables may be more than using cheap ground beef. Certainly the final product is much lighter, more delicious and nutritionally balanced too.

1 lamb chop
2 lbs. ground beef
1/4 cup grated onions
2 tsp. salt
1/4 cup fresh breadcrumbs
2 tbs. milk to soak the crumbs
1 tbs. soy sauce mixed in milk

1 strip bacon, partially cooked,
   finely chopped
1/4 cup grated carrots
1 egg, unbeaten
1 cup breadcrumbs, for coating
1 egg, lightly beaten for coating crumbs
oil for deep-frying

Broil lamb chop. Remove meat from bone and finely chop or grind it. Combine lamb with all remaining ingredients except breadcrumbs, 1 beaten egg and oil. Form into 1-inch balls. Coat the balls with crumbs, beaten egg and crumbs again. Heat oil in wok to 325°F. Fry for one minute. Meatballs can also be baked in a pan (leave space between the balls) in the oven at 350°F. for about 15 minutes. Actual time required in oven varies. Test them for doneness. Meatballs won't be as round as when deep fried.

There was a cook who was always very cautious in order to do a perfect job. He made one dozen meatballs. He cut three balls to see if they were done, another three to see if they were overdone, and tasted three for their seasoning. That left him with a pair of perfect balls to be served. The count is correct because one ball was so hot it burned the perfectionist's fingers and dropped on the floor!

CANTON SPARERIBS

Spareribs are an all time favorite but we have to change the cooking method so the final product will be more suitable as an appetizer.

12 center-cut ribs, 3 inches long
3 tbs. soy sauce
1 clove garlic, mashed
3 tbs. honey

3 tbs. dry white wine
1 cup pineapple juice
light cooking oil

Using a small pointed knife, loosen about an inch of meat from one end of each rib by running knife between the meat and bone. Push loosened meat to the opposite end so rib will now have a ball-of-meat on one end and a bare bone on the other. The bare bone should be wrapped with a fancy paper when served. Place prepared ribs on a plate and steam in wok for 15 minutes (see **Steaming Racks,** page 131). Remove ribs. Drain and dry wok. Combine soy sauce, garlic, honey and wine in wok. Add steamed ribs to mixture. Turn to coat well. Simmer over medium-low heat about 30 minutes or until tender. Bring pineapple juice to a boil. Dip each rib into hot juice just before serving. Drain ribs thoroughly and brush with heated cooking oil to make them shiny.

BEEF JERKY BOWTIES

(About 80 Pieces)

2 lbs. bottom round, cut 1/4 inch thick
1/2 cup dry vermouth
1 tbs. lemon juice
oil for frying

Quenching Mixture:
1 cup pineapple juice
1/2 cup soy sauce
2 tbs. honey

Be sure meat is no more than 1/4-inch thick. Trim outside fat from slices of meat. Marinate in vermouth and lemon juice overnight. When ready to make bowties, pound marinated meat with a mallet to flatten evenly. Cut slices into 3 x 2-inch strips. Make a lengthwise slit about 1-inch long in the middle of each strip. Tuck one end of each strip back through the slit. Pull and shape neatly into a bowtie. Mix quenching ingredients in mixing bowl and set aside. Pour oil into wok to a depth of about 1-inch. Heat to 300°F. Fry bowties until they shrink and brown. Remove from wok and plunge into quenching mixture. (See more about quenching on page 109.) Leave in mixture for one minute. Drain on rack. Taste the first piece for flavor. You still have time for adjusting the quenching mixture. Add more pineapple juice to reduce saltiness or soy sauce for a stronger flavor. You can also make it more fragrant by sprinkling a little Five-Fragrant-Spice Powder on top just before serving warm or at room temperature. Note: See page 90 for folding instructions.

BEEF COINS

A 2-1/2 to 3 pound, center-cut piece of beef shank is needed for this recipe. Since beef shank is usually cut into slices for making soup, you will have to ask your friendly butcher to cut the ends off a whole shank leaving about a 6-inch center piece. Then all of the meat should be pulled away from the bone in whole, long pieces with membranes intact. When properly prepared, the slices will have pretty patterns like coins and taste delicious. There will be considerable shrinkage—just like our coins.

1 whole piece beef shank
6 tbs. light soy sauce per each 2 lbs., **plus**
1 tbs. honey, **and**
1/2 tsp. Five Spice Powder

With a sharp knife, make a cut along the shank bone. Pull and cut the meat away in whole pieces. Place pieces of meat, soy sauce, honey and spices in heavy saucepan or wok. On low heat, simmer uncovered for one or two hours or until tender, depending on the heat source and the cookware. During the simmering, the meat will release its own natural juices. Turn meat every thirty minutes for even doneness and color.

Don't hesitate to try this appetizer. It's not difficult, can be made ahead and is delicious.

Test by piercing with one chopstick or a fork. Be sure pieces of meat are very tender as they will become very firm, almost tough, when chilled. When done, most of the liquid will be gone. If not, you can reduce the liquid by raising the heat to evaporate it away. Only a few minutes will be required, so don't go away. It will burn easily. Chill meat. When firm, cut into "coins" and serve with fancy toothpicks.

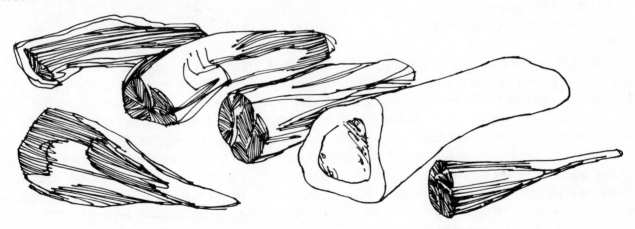

ANGEL FINGERS

Instant Dough
2 cups instant mashed potato mix
2 tbs. cornstarch
2 tbs. all-purpose flour
2 tsp. salt
1/4 tsp. white pepper
1 cup warmed chicken broth

1/2 lb. ground beef mixed with
   1 tbs. cornstarch
1/2 tsp. salt
pinch of onion powder
1-1/2 cups fresh moist breadcrumbs
3 lightly beaten eggs
oil for deep-frying

Warm a mixing bowl slightly by pouring hot water into it. Let it stand for a minute or two and discard water and pat bowl dry. Add first five ingredients to bowl. Gradually add heated broth, stirring constantly. Mixture will form a ball of dough. If it seems too soft, add a little more cornstarch. Dry-cook ground beef (using no oil in wok) over medium heat. Add 1/2 teaspoon salt and onion powder. Mix well. Beef will form a ball as it cooks because of the cornstarch. Cool beef completely. Pinch off ping pong ball-size pieces of dough. With oiled hands, flatten dough to about 1/8 inch thickness, in the shape of an oval. Place about a teaspoon of filling into each dough oval. Roll into a finger shape. Roll in breadcrumbs, beaten egg and breadcrumbs

A food processor makes light and fluffy breadcrumbs — perfect for this recipe.

again. Reshape in hand gently and press crumbs on. Fry in wok in oil at 350°F. until Angel Fingers turn golden brown. These may be reheated. Simply place cooked Fingers on a baking sheet and heat in 350°F. oven for about 12 minutes.

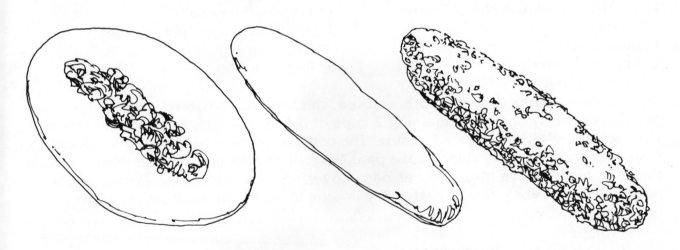

CHICKEN FRITTERS

This easy appetizer can be partially prepared ahead, then dipped in batter and fried just before serving.

4 cups chicken broth
1/2 cup finely minced raw chicken
 breast
1/2 cup chicken fat
1/2 cup cornstarch

1/4 tsp. salt
1/4 tsp. white pepper
3 cups Nine-Three-One* Batter
 (see page 35)
oil for frying

Combine 2 cups chicken broth, chicken, chicken fat, cornstarch, salt and pepper. Mix thoroughly. Bring the remaining 2 cups of broth to a boil. Add the first mixture. Stir vigorously and boil for one minute. The consistency will be that of thick pudding. Pour into an oiled, 8 by 8-inch cake pan. Mixture should be no more than 3/4 inch thick. Pour any extra into another pan. Cover and chill until firm. When ready to serve, cut into cubes. Dip in batter. Fry in wok in 350°F. oil until crust is firm and a light golden brown.

*For 3 cups of batter, double the recipe.

NINE-THREE-ONE BATTER
(egg-shell type)

(1-1/2 Cups)

This batter will form a thin, crispy and light crust. It enlarges the size of fried food without adding too much weight. You can easily remember this batter, since its measurements are reduced by one-third in logical order: flour, cornstach and oil, plus about the same amount of lukewarm water as flour.

9 tbs. (1 cup plus 1 tbs.) self-rising
  flour
3 tbs. cornstarch

1 tbs. vegetable oil or chicken fat
9 tbs. (approximately) lukewarm water

Mix the first three items in large bowl. Add water slowly and gently stir to a smooth batter. Let it rest for five minutes before using. Dip the food to be fried in the batter. (DON'T OVER-DO!) Let excess batter drip back into bowl. Fry in wok in oil at 325°F., or as indicated by the recipe. In most cases, watching for a lovely golden color is more reliable than timing the frying by minutes.

This recipe is easy to double, triple or even quadruple.

PETITE DRUMSTICKS

Here are directions and illustrations for turning chicken wings into drumsticks—very petite indeed.

1 lb. chicken fryer wings,
  about 12 wings
1/2 tsp. salt
1 pinch white pepper and
  onion powder

Nine-Three-One Batter,
  (see page 35)
1 beaten egg
breadcrumbs
oil for deep-frying

Cut the wings into three parts, **through** the two joints. It should be effortless or you are missing the joints. Discard wing tips. The ends which link the middle and upper sections of the wing have soft bones. Trim these ends with a sharp knife, cutting off about one-eighth of an inch. Using two pieces of paper towel, fold each twice into a four layer square. Hold a paper towel square between the thumb and first and second fingers of each hand. This is to protect your fingertips and add more friction when you do the next operation. With one hand, hold the large piece of wing section at the smaller end. Rest the larger end on top of a chopping block in a vertical posi-

Continued

tion. Holding tightly at the top end, push down the meat and skin at the same time, to the point where the bone is fully exposed. Normally, it will not be hard to do this job, but you might want to pre-loosen the top-end of the wing with a small knife before you start. For the middle section of the wing, the section between the wing tip and upper part of wing, do the same as above. When the top end reveals the bones (there are two bones in this section of wing), use a small knife and cut through the ligament. Now keep pushing the meat (while you are holding tightly) as mentioned above. Now pay attention, one of the two tiny bones is thinner. You must work on this thinner bone or you will get into trouble—you better believe it! Holding this section of wing, use one hand to hold the meat, the other hand to hold the tip of the thinner bone. Turn this bone upside down—180°. Bring the thinner bone's tip back to the chopping block, in a vertical position. Push the whole section of wing downward. Since the thinner bone's tip is against the block, it has no where to go but out through the meat and alongside the larger bone again. Now you will find it easy to remove the thinner bone from the meat! Season the wing sections with salt, pepper and onion powder. Refrigerate for an hour or overnight. Do you still need an explanation about how to finish the coating and frying? (See page 35.)

CHICKEN BALLS

(60 Pieces)

Late one evening when I was helping in the restaurant's kitchen, we were running short on raw food. One customer asked for a Beijing dish of boneless chicken in large chunks. The order called for eight large pieces and we were two chunks short. However, we had enough diced chicken, so I "glued" them together with a binding mixture to form two large chunks.

It worked out nicely. Later, the customer told me the texture was even more tender! Because of this incident, I came up with this recipe.

2 cups diced skinless raw chicken
2 tsp. salt
1 pinch each of sugar, pepper and onion powder
Nine-Three-One Batter, (see page 35)
oil for deep-frying
1 tbs. finely chopped green onion

Mix diced chicken and seasonings. Let stand at room temperature for 15 minutes. Gently fold chicken into Nine-Three-One Batter. Heat oil in wok to 325°F.

over medium heat. Take about one teaspoon of mixture on an oiled spoon. Use another oiled spoon to carefully push the mixture into hot oil. Be careful not to make the ball too large because the outside will be overcooked before the inside is done. Fry until the crust is golden brown. Sprinkle with chopped green onion and another pinch of pepper before serving.

CHICKEN OF A THOUSAND LEGS

One of the many buddhas is the Buddha of a Thousand Hands. This recipe's name is derived from the same concept.

2 to 2-1/2 lbs. chicken parts
1 quart water
1 tbs. salt
1/2 tsp. white pepper
1 tbs. oil
1/4 cup minced onion
1 clove garlic, crushed
1 tbs. light soy sauce
5 to 6 cups self-rising flour
3 cups fresh breadcrumbs
3 beaten eggs
oil for frying

Place chicken in large saucepan or Dutch oven. Add water, salt and pepper. Cover and bring to a boil. Reduce heat and simmer 40 minutes, or until done. Remove from heat. Remove chicken from broth and allow to cool to lukewarm. While chicken is still warm (much easier than when it's cold), remove and discard skin and fat. Tear meat into small, short shreds and set aside. In wok, heat oil to medium temperature. Add onion and garlic and cook, while stirring, until golden brown. Stir in chicken and soy sauce. Remove from heat and set aside. Measure reserved broth. Add enough water to make it 1 quart. In large pan, such as a 2-quart stockpot, bring broth to a boil. Reduce heat to low. Add the flour gradually by a hand-held sieve. Stir constantly. Add only enough flour to form a soft dough. It may not be necessary to use all the flour. Remove from heat, cover with towel and set aside to cool. Take about 1 tablespoon of dough and flatten it into an oval in the palm of your hand. It should be thin and about 3 inches by 2 inches in size. Place about 1-1/2 teaspoons of the chicken mixture in the center of the dough. Fold to enclose filling. Mold into a chicken drumstick shape. They should be small and delicate in size. If desired, "drumsticks" may be covered and refrigerated at this point for up to 2 days prior to cooking. Just before frying, roll "drumsticks" in breadcrumbs, egg and breadcrumbs again. Deep fry in a wok in oil at 350°F. for 2 minutes or more, or until golden brown. Drain on paper towels. To serve, pierce from the thin end with a fancy toothpick.

This recipe can easily be doubled.

(48 Pieces) # TOFU BALLS

Tofu is the Chinese name for soy bean curd. It has several varieties, determined mainly by its water content, so its texture can be classified as firm, soft or very soft. Only the firm type should be used for appetizers.

2 boxes (14 ozs. each) firm tofu
2 eggs
1 tsp. salt
1/4 cup finely chopped cooked ham
2 tbs. cornstarch

Drain the tofu. Mash it, then wrap in a dish towel. Twist the towel to remove excess water from tofu. Mix mashed tofu with the remaining ingredients. Shape mixture into 1-inch balls. Place on an oiled plate. Steam in wok over medium heat for 15 minutes. It may be necessary to do this in several batches. Drain steamed balls on towels. Serve with a dipping sauce from pages 68 or 69, if desired.

DEEP FRIED TOFU CUBES

(24 Cubes)

This is a very easy and delicious recipe that is perfrect for an appetizer.

1 box (14 ozs.) firm tofu
1 tbs. salt
oil for deep frying
1 tbs. soy sauce
1 tbs. oil
1 cup seasoned chicken broth (homemade or Swanson's)
1 tbs. cornstarch mixed with 2 tbs. water

Drain tofu. Cut into 1/2-inch cubes. Place cubes in a large bowl. Cover with water and add the tablespoon of salt. Leave at room temperature for an hour. This is to firm the outside of cubes for deep-frying. Drain and dry cubes thoroughly before frying. Deep-fry in wok in oil at 350°F. until cubes are golden grown. Drain well. Combine remaining ingredients in saucepan. Cook, stirring, until thickened. Serve sauce in bowl for dipping cubes.

BEEF PUFFS

This is a classic Chinese recipe, but my stuffing method is revolutionary. Usually we stuff the deep fried cubes through a slit on one side, but this special method of turning the cubes inside out makes them crunchy, inside and out. Before making Beef Puffs, you have to make the Deep-Fried Tofu Cubes on page 45. They are softer and easier to turn and stuff if they are made the day before.

24 Deep-Fried Tofu Cubes, page 45
1 tbs. oil
1 cup (about 1/2 lb.) lean ground beef
1 tbs. soy sauce

pinch sugar and white pepper
1 tbs. cornstarch
oil for deep frying

Prepare the Deep-Fried Cubes the day before, if possible. When ready to stuff, carefully turn them inside out. Heat 1 tablespoon oil in wok. Add ground beef and cook until pink is gone. Drain off any liquid that accumulates. Stir in remaining ingredients, except oil for frying. Stuff the beef mixture into the concave part of the Deep-Fried Cubes. Deep fry Beef Puffs in wok in 325°F. oil for one minute. Drain before serving. Makes 24 puffs.

Red Eggs Story

There is a Chinese tradition that when a baby survives to the third month a party is given and red-tinted boiled eggs are distributed for a celebration. Forget the unjustified nonsense about odd numbers for girls and even numbers for boys. In fact, in ancient times, mothers were the heads of families and children took their mother's name. Women were always respected and it was not necessary to reveal their marital status. The respectful title of "Woman Scholar" is still used now, instead of the meaningless "Ms." Married women may use their own parents' name, a privilege they did not fight for, and there was no bra to burn, as they never wore them! It had long been observed that baby girls have better potential of surviving; therefore, if the first boy died in his youth, the second boy (his parents being concerned that events might repeat themselves) purposely gave him a girlish name for good luck.

One day I returned home from a baby's party. For unknown reason I put some red eggs in my freezer. Oh, it was a joyful party which I do remember!

Days later, when I wanted to use the eggs, I found the texture had been changed. Bubbles formed in the egg white, making it resemble a sponge and this inspired me to create a dish. I followed an idea for a frozen bean curd dish in Northern China. I called my new dish Eskimo Eggs.

ESKIMO EGGS

There is no Eskimo chicken, so your friends might ask you "Where did you get the Eskimo Eggs?" You may say: "Once upon a time, a charming lady gave a baby to her handsome man, the man gave a party for their baby, the cute baby gave some eggs to Gary; and Gary gave these eggs to me and I am giving them to you!"

It sounds like Dean Martin is singing: ". . . Everybody NEEDS somebody, some time . . ."

12 eggs, hard boiled and frozen
3 cups water

3 tbs. soy sauce
1 tbs. oil

Because each freezer is different in coldness, you have to inspect the eggs after 2 days. Pick one egg, leave it in the water to thaw, shell it and check. If the egg white is turning yellowish and transparent, that is about right; if not, keep freezing them for a few more days. Don't freeze too long, however, or the white will get flaky. Combine water, soy sauce and oil in a wok. Place the shelled eggs in wok (after they reach the proper point) and simmer for 1 hour and serve. You'll be surprised at how much smoother the yolk is now! To serve as an appetizer, cut the eggs in quarters.

TEA EGGS

This recipe is a good example for showing that directions in cooking should be followed, or the chemistry of the ingredients will change during cooking. Eggs prepared in this manner have a pretty pattern, similar to cracked old porcelain.

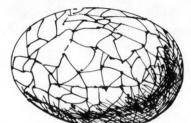

1 qt. water and 2 black tea bags
1 dozen eggs
3 tbs. soy sauce
1 tsp. sugar
1 tsp. Five-Spice Powder

Simmer water and tea bags for 10 minutes, then cool. Add eggs and slowly bring to a boil. Cook five minutes. Remove eggs, crack the shells all over with a metal teaspoon, but don't remove shells. Put eggs back into the tea along with the rest of the seasonings. Boil for another 10 minutes then leave overnight. When ready to serve, shell eggs and cut each one into four wedges. Serve hot or cold.

STUFFED EGGS

(Makes 24)

12 small eggs, hard-cooked
2 strips bacon, soft-cooked and diced
Binding Mixture, page 16
1-1/2 cups fresh breadcrumbs (see page 16)

Slice the hard-cooked eggs in half lengthwise. Remove yolks. Mash yolks with bacon. Stuff yolk mixture back into white halves. Brush entire egg with Binding Mixture. Roll in breadcrumbs. Broil until golden brown.

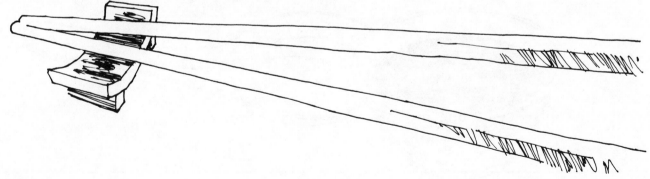

Square Eggs In Shell

There is a gadget on the market that will press a shelled, hard-cooked egg into a square! I had one; and I don't want to buy a dozen, as it is rather expensive.

An old Chinese magic book said: "immerse the eggs in strong vinegar for several days until the acid dissolves the egg shells' calcium." By then the shell is somehow soft enought to re-shape into flat bottoms and tops. Square eggs in a shell! Terrible news for hens!

This is an interesting trick but not very useful, as it really causes too much work and time. So, on the next page is a classic Chinese recipe, which without using food color, turns cooked eggs a lovely jade color.

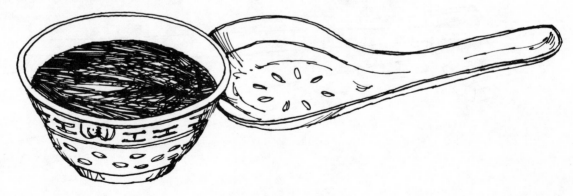

JADE EGGS

(12 Eggs)

When I was a young boy, our family cook, Old Tin, taught me how to make these special eggs. The baking soda causes the eggs to turn a lovely shade of pale green and expand while cooking, so don't fill the egg shells more than hall full. The eggs must be cooked over low heat. High heat will cause them to explode!

12 eggs
1/2 tsp. baking soda
1/2 cup strong chicken broth

1 tsp. salt
1 tbs. vegetable oil

Carefully put a round hole in the egg shells at the smaller end, using chopsticks or something about three-eights inch in diameter. Shake out the egg white and yolk. You can make this easier if you insert a chopstick first and pierce the yolk. Gently rinse and clean the shells. Drain, hole down, for 10 minutes. Beat the eggs. Add remaining ingredients and beat well. Fill the egg shells half full with egg mixture. Rip some pieces of thin white paper about a half inch larger than the holes in egg shells. Soak them in what remains of the egg for about 2 minutes. Use these scraps of paper to seal the holes in the egg shells. Arrange eggs, hole up, on a rack in wok and steam at 200°F. for about 20 minutes. Remove shell and serve hot or cold.

(48 Pieces) # SILVER AND GOLDEN EGGS

This recipe is filling, ideal for young people who always seem to be hungry. It can be prepared ahead of time, which is helpful for large parties.

12 small hard-cooked eggs
1/4 cup Binding Mixture, page 16
6 strips raw bacon, finely chopped
1 cup ground beef

Instant Dough, page 32
pinch pepper, salt to taste
1-1/2 cups fresh breadcrumbs
   (see page 16)
oil for frying

Cut eggs in half **lengthwise.** Brush them with Binding Mixture, reserving half of mixture for later use. Partially cook bacon; it should be soft. Add ground beef and cook until brown. Remove from heat and cool. Prepare dough. Mix ground beef and bacon into dough. Taste and add pepper and salt. Using the dough mixture, shape egg halves to form a whole egg. Brush with remaining Binding Mixture. Roll in breadcrumbs. Heat oil in wok to 325°F. Fry crumb-coated eggs until golden brown. Cut in half **crosswise** for serving. Each half should contain egg and dough—silver and gold!

If desired, omit bacon and instant dough. Mix raw ground beef with salt and pepper. Use this mixture to shape egg halves. Finish as directed.

EGGS IN NESTS

(Makes 24)

He thought small and created a wonderland with all construction scaled down — Walt Disney. Here is a Chinese appetizer which is also small and elegant.

24 bread rounds, each 1-1/2 inches
   in diameter
1 cup Binding Mixture, page 16
2 cups finely ground shrimp
1 tsp salt.

1 pinch white pepper and onion powder
breadcrumbs
1 can hard-cooked quail eggs
oil for frying

Brush the bread rounds with Binding Mixture. Combine ground shrimp and seasonings. Shape and pile the seasoned shrimp on top of bread rounds (see To Form a Hemisphere, page 98). Coat the shrimp with breadcrumbs. Place an egg in the middle and press it down leaving part of the egg still exposed. Deep fry in wok at 325°F. for one minute, or until the bread is golden brown. Drain and serve warm. NOTE: quail eggs are available in Chinese grocery stores. Each can has 24 tiny eggs. The price is about the same as for a dozen of fresh chicken eggs. Fresh uncooked quail eggs are sometimes sold on Sundays or Holidays in Chinatown, San Francisco.

If desired, eggs can be cut in half and recipe doubled.

LAUGHING CLAMS

(12 to 15)

In this recipe, the clams are served in their shells, with a stuffing. Because the shells are wide open, they look as though they are laughing!

Although this recipe was devised to make 12 servings, I have called for 15 clams. This is to insure at least 12 will open. We must leave room for sad clams, too.

15 small, fresh clams, scrubbed clean
1 tbs. oil
1 clove mashed garlic
1/2 cup ground pork
1 tbs. soy sauce
1 tsp. sugar
1 tsp. sesame oil
1 beaten egg
1 tbs. breadcrumbs
1 tsp. cornstarch

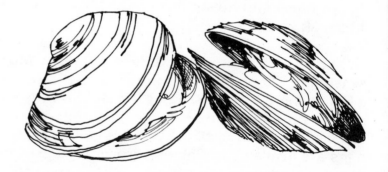

Place a small amount of water in a wok. Add clams and steam just until they open. Discard any unopened clams. Remove clams from shells and set aside. Reserve shells and clam liquor. Rinse and dry wok. Heat oil to medium temperature in wok. Add garlic, stir 2 minutes. Add pork and cook until it loses its pink color. Stir in clam liquor, soy sauce, sugar and sesame oil. Remove from heat and let cool. Stir in remaining ingredients. Pat clam shells dry and brush inside of shell with oil. Divide stuffing among 12 shells. Half bury one clam in each shell. Place clams in wok, being careful not to spill stuffing. Cover and cook over medium-high heat for about 8 minutes, or until stuffing is firm. For this part of the recipe, the wok is serving as an oven. If you are preparing a quantity of Laughing Clams for a large party, bake in a 250°F. oven for 10 minutes.

(40 Cubes)

ROCK COD CUBES

We expect to serve appetizers with fancy toothpicks or use our fingers. The fried fish the English call Fish & Chips is not a very suitable appetizer. Here is a modified version that is.

1 lb. fillet of rock cod
pinch white pepper
1/4 cup all-purpose flour
1 tsp. salt

pinch onion powder
1 egg yolk + 1 whole egg
oil for frying

Cut the cod into bite-size cubes. Season with pepper, salt and onion powder and let stand at room temperature for 5 minutes. Roll the cubes in flour; then dip in beaten eggs and again coat with flour. Fry immediately in wok in oil at 325°F. until the crust is golden brown.

ROLLING SOLE

Because sole is much thinner, a different preparation and cooking method should be used. It is simple enough to·puff up its size by using the Nine-Three-One Batter.

1 lb. fillet of sole
1 tsp. salt
1 pinch white pepper

1 pinch onion powder
Nine-Three-One Batter, page 35
oil for deep-frying

Cut sole into 1 inch by 3 inch pieces. Season with salt, pepper and onion powder and let stand at room temperature 5 minutes. Dip into batter and deep fry in wok at 325°F. until the crust is golden brown. You may use the double-frying method with this recipe to avoid the last minute rush at serving time. That is, in advance, fry until the color is pale-yellowish. Then fry again just before serving, a matter of about 15 seconds, in oil heated to 350°F.

FISH PING PONG

If you are asked about this recipe say: "In 1970, Kissinger secretly went to China and brought back this recipe—his mission was completed under the code of Ping Pong Diplomacy!"

enough vegetable shortening for
   20 balls of butterball size
cornstarch
2 lbs. fillet of sole, diced
2 tsp. salt

2 egg whites
1 pinch white pepper
2 tbs. evaporated milk
1 tbs. oil, used in water for boiling

Chill shortening. Using a butterball scoop, form chilled shortening into balls. Roll

them in cornstarch-dusted pan by holding the pan just above the countertop. Swiftly make a circular motion with the pan. The centrifugal force will cause the balls to roll and bump against the side of the pan. Roll until balls are lightly coated with cornstarch. Chill for an hour. Reserve pan for later use. Blend diced fillet of sole at high speed in a blender or food processor. Gradually add seasoning and remaining ingredients. Continue blending until the mixture turns into a fine paste. To shape, place one heaping tablespoonful (use measuring tablespoon) of paste in your palm. Pick up one chilled shortening ball and fold the paste carefully, but rather roughly, around it making it into a larger ball. Chill finished balls for another hour, placing them in a tray with space between balls. Using the same cornstarch-dusted pan used earlier, try to improve the roundness of balls by rolling once again in cornstarch. Have a pan of pre-boiled water at least five inches deep, with one tablespoonful of oil added. Turn off heat so that the water is motionless. Drop balls into water. After all balls are in the pan, raise heat to medium-high and slowly bring it to a simmer, cook balls for two minutes. During this time, some balls will surface. Gently push them down with a slotted cooking spoon. When all balls have surfaced, raise heat to high, bring the water to the boiling point, and stop! Remove balls onto a cookie rack. Pierce each ver-

Continued

tically from top through bottom with a toothpick. Remove the toothpick. The holes should enable the melted shortening to drain out of the balls, slowly and thoroughly. Watch those lazy balls which don't drain, and unclog the holes or turn the balls over. Before serving, place balls in a skillet at medium heat. Move the skillet back and forth without lifting from heat source until balls are warm and more of the shortening has drained from them. Presto! Hollow fishballs. Now is your moment of truth! Conceal the holes with a fancy toothpick through each ball, placing ball in the middle of the toothpick. Explain when you serve: "Chinese use a single chopstick to practice ping pong instead of a paddle. These appetizers are served only to players who have pierced a ping pong ball with a single chopstick!"

SOY SAUCED SQUID

Squid should be cooked very quickly or it will become tough. If you should over-cook it, all is not lost. Continue simmering it until it becomes tender again, about 30 minutes.

1 lb. small squid
2 cups water
2 tbs. soy sauce

1 tsp. sugar
1 tsp. sesame oil
1 tbs. dry white wine

Clean squid by grasping body firmly in hands. Pull off head, tentacles and ink sac. Discard head and ink sac. Save tentacles and cut into 1-inch pieces. Pull out and discard transparent backbone. Squeeze any remaining material from inside body and discard. Wash squid thoroughly. Cut body into 1/2-inch rings. Combine remaining ingredients in wok. Heat to boiling. Add squid and simmer 1/2 minute. (Don't over-cook.) Transfer to a bowl. Cover and refrigerate overnight. When ready to serve, strain sauce into small dish. Serve squid accompanied by sauce for dipping.

(About 12 Pieces) FRIED SHRIMP CHINESE STYLE

There are many restaurants that serve a Combination Seafood Plate with fried shrimp. However, by using my egg shell-type batter, the shrimp will be much lighter.

1/2 lb. (about 12) medium shrimp
1/2 tsp. salt

1 pinch white pepper and onion powder
Nine-Three-One Batter, page 35

Shell shrimp, leaving tails. Devein, rinse and dry. Sprinkle with salt and pepper. Dip into Nine-Three-One Batter (did you rest it?) by holding the tails of the shrimp. Heat oil in wok to 325°F. Lay shrimp gently in the oil one at a time. Do not crowd shrimp or they will stick together. Flip shrimp when the crust starts to firm, not before. Normally, it will be twenty seconds after you lay the shrimp in the oil. Leave them for another 20 seconds, to firm the other side.

(24 Pieces)

DRAGON ON THE JADE TREE

The shrimp will fit tightly around the broccoli after they are cooked.

24 medium shrimp
1 tsp. salt
1 pinch white pepper
1 pinch sugar
1 egg white, lightly beaten

1 tbs. cornstarch
24 broccoli stems, each 2 inches long
1 quart water, to which 1 tbs. salt and
    1 tbs. vegetable oil have been added

Shell, devein and rinse shrimp. Dry with paper towels. Mix together salt, pepper, sugar, egg white and cornstarch. Brush shrimp with egg white mixture. Split ends of broccoli with a cross-cut (see Basic Information, page 17). Wrap shrimp around broccoli stems. Shrimp will fit tightly after they cook and shrink slightly. Bring water mixture to a boil. Reduce heat to simmer. Lay the assembled shrimp and broccoli on a plate. Set plate on rack in wok over simmering water. Cover and steam about 5 minutes. Be careful not to overcook, as it will toughen the shrimp. Gently remove the appetizers from water and drain briefly on paper towels. Serve with toothpicks and your choice of Dipping Sauces on pages 68 and 69. May be served warm or cold.

DIPPING SAUCES

Someone once commented that the English have one sauce: mint, and hundreds of religions, while the French have one religion: Catholic and hundreds of sauces. The great master Confucius taught a middle course, so the Chinese have many religions and many sauces. The recipes here are simplified espeically for my readers.

Sweet and Sour Sauce   **(3/4 Cup)**

3 tbs. orange juice
1 tbs. cornstarch
3 tbs. sugar
1 tbs. dark soy sauce

3 tbs. malt vinegar
3 tbs. catsup
1 tbs. oil

Mix orange juice and cornstarch together until smooth. Set aside. Combine remaining ingredients in saucepan over medium heat. When hot, add cornstarch mixture. Stir until thickened.

Pungent Dipping Sauce (1/2 Cup)

3 tbs. light soy sauce
1 tsp. sugar
3 tbs. cold water

1 tsp. sesame oil
1 tsp. malt vinegar
3 to 6 drops red chili oil

Combine all ingredients except chili oil. Mix well. Add chili oil drop by drop until desired degree of "hotness" is reached.

Oyster Dipping Sauce (1/3 Cup)

3 tbs. oyster sauce
3 tbs. water
1 tsp. sesame oil

Combine all ingredients.

(12 Rolls)

ARMY AND NAVY

Ham and shrimp are used in this recipe, representing land and sea, a fancy appetizer honoring our Army and Navy.

12 slices very fresh thin sandwich bread, trimmed of crusts

24 strips ham, 1/4 inch wide—use sliced sandwich ham cut equal length to the width of trimmed bread

1 cup Binding Mixture, page 16

12 medium size shrimp, shelled and halved

1/4 tsp. salt

1 pinch each sugar, pepper and onion powder

oil for deep-frying

Place the trimmed bread in front of you, the narrow side placed vertically. The side near you is the south side. Brush the bread, shrimp and ham all over with Binding Mixture. Lay one strip of ham on the south edge. Top it with two halves of shrimp, each with narrow part pointing to the center, and the large ends of shrimp neatly flush with the east and west edges of the bread. Lay another strip of ham on top of shrimp. To roll sandwich, cut a square of plastic wrap an inch larger than the trimmed bread. Place the wrap under the bread, assemble the meat as above, start to roll from

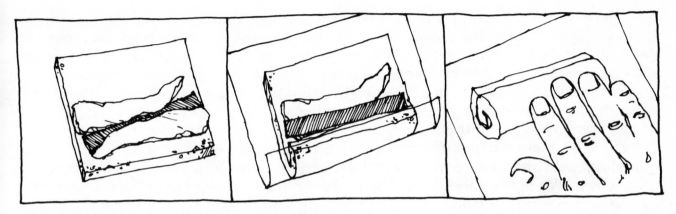

the south toward the north. Using plastic wrap, go through the whole rolling procedure. Now, gently unroll it, remove the plastic wrap, then re-roll the bread to form a tight roll. Seal the fold properly by brushing it with the Binding Mixture. You don't need a new piece of plastic wrap for the next roll, unless it gets crinkled too much. Place the finished rolls on a towel with fold facing down until you are ready to fry them. Heat oil in wok to 325°F. Fry appetizers until the color is a beautiful light golden brown.

(20 Dumplings) # SMILING FISH

There were ten cooking contests held during San Francisco's First Annual Fair & Expo, in June 1982, at the Moscone Convention Center. As Resource Developer for Self-Help for the Elderly, a non-profit agency, I lead several projects. One is known as the "Smiling Butler" Catering Service. An hour before the deadline for the contest, I was tempted to compete in the Dim Sum Division but I had nothing ready. Thanks to many 'helping feet' dashing to get items needed, an entry by an anonymous "Smiling Butler" was ready when the seven judges arrived precisely on time. It won the First Prize by a big margin of points over the second place winner which was also a shrimp dumpling, but I had made my dumplings into tiny fish and won many points for uniqueness. When the Blue Ribbon was awarded, the "Smiling Butler" was revealed. I can be seen wearing my funny smile and holding a plateful of Smiling Fish on page 2.

Shrimp Dumplings, page 134
frozen peas and carrots and whole kernel corn

Prepare dough and filling as directed for Shrimp Dumplings. Stuff and shape as illustrated on the opposite page. Use the colorful vegetables for eyes. Steam as directed in recipe.

SLEEPING MERMAIDS
UNDER THE CANDLELIGHT

(4 Servings)

In one Chinese fairytale, Neptune gave a party for his mermaids. After a lot of wine, dance and song, the mermaids fell asleep under the candlelight . . .

1 lb. large shrimp
1 cup seasoned chicken broth
1 tbs. dry vermouth
1 envelope unflavored gelatin

1 bottle semi-dry champagne
4 champagne glasses
4 birthday cake candles, spiral type
1 bunch fresh cilantro

Shell and devein shrimp. Lay them flat on a plate. Set plate on rack in wok. Steam on high for 10 minutes. Let it cool. Heat broth and dissolve gelatin. When it is cool, mix with half cup of chilled champagne. Drain steamed shrimp on a dry plate. Lay close together, but not touching each other. Pour the gelatin mixture over shirmp just to cover. Chill until firm. Run a knife tip in between shrimp. Leave the gelatin attached randomly to shrimp. Arrange them on the tips of fancy toothpicks. Shorten the spiral candles to three inches long. Heat the candle bottoms and let the melted wax glue them in the centers of champagne glasses. When ready to serve, arrange the shrimp around the candles with snipped cilantro in between. Fill each glass with champagne and light the candles.

SESAME SHRIMP

In conventional Chinese cooking, the finishing touch of a dish is to sprinkle some cooking wine and sesame oil on it. Both will add a pleasant flavor to almost any dish. Sesame oil will not be very useful in making appetizers, but sesame seed will create many interesting ones—fancy and flavorful. You might have to visit a Chinese store to get black and white sesame seed, mixed in a ratio of 5 parts white to 1 part black.

about 3/4 lb. cooked shrimp
1 egg white
bread
2 strips bacon, finely chopped

1 tbs. cornstarch
about 10 slices fresh bread
1 cup sesame seed
oil for frying

Finely chop shrimp. Mix with egg white, bacon and cornstarch. Chill for 30 minutes. Trim crusts from bread. Cut bread to whatever shape you like, preferably an odd shape, different from the rest of the appetizers so it will be distinctive—be creative! Pile a small amount of shrimp mixture on bread. Press seeds onto the mixture firmly so they will stick when fried. Heat oil in wok to 325°F. Fry appetizers until the white seeds are lightly brown.

BUTTERFLY SHRIMP

(27 Pieces)

Simple to prepare and always appreciated by guests.

1 lb. shrimp, about 27 pieces
1 tsp. salt
1 pinch white pepper
1 pinch onion powder

2 eggs, lightly beaten
1 cup breadcrumbs
oil for frying

Prepare shrimp (see Basic Information, page 22,) but leave tails intact. Devein deeply but do not cut shrimp all the way through. Gently flatten shrimp with the side of a cleaver or mallet. Combine salt, pepper and onion powder. Sprinkle over shrimp. Coat the seasoned shrimp with breadcrumbs. Dip into beaten eggs, then again into breadcrumbs. Flatten again very gently before frying. Heat oil in wok to 300°F. Fry breaded shrimp until the crust is a light golden brown. Watching the color of the shrimp is a more reliable test of doneness than counting the time. Be sure to keep the oil at 300°F. Serve with lemon wedges. Let guests season with lemon juice—tastes delicious!

NEPTUNE'S SHRIMP

This recipe uses the tiny bread cubes described on the following page. Once you try it, you'll understand how to apply the cubes to other appetizers to make them extra fancy.

20 whole large shrimp
1/2 tsp. salt
1 cup shrimp, ground to paste
3 strips bacon, finely chopped

1 pinch each sugar and white pepper
1 cup Binding Mixture, page 16
about 2 cups tiny bread cubes, page 79
oil for frying

Shell shrimp but leave the tails intact. Devein and slit the backs deep enough to hold stuffing. Combine salt, ground shrimp, bacon, sugar and pepper. Brush whole shrimp with Binding Mixture then fill the slit neatly with stuffing. Coat with tiny bread cubes. If the shrimp are not fully covered with tiny bread cubes, no harm done. You may repair them by dipping the cubes into the Binding Mixture, then filling in the uncovered spaces. Heat oil in wok to 325°F. Fry shrimp until the bread cubes are light golden brown.

TINY BREAD CUBES

We use very tiny fresh bread cubes instead of fresh breadcrumbs because they are uniform in shape. Because they are made from flattened pieces of bread, their texture is also different from breadcrumbs. When used on deep-fried foods, the final product is much crisper.

It's easy to make these tiny cubes. First, flatten a piece of white bread with a rolling pin. Then trim and discard all the crusts. Cut each piece of bread into 16 strips. Cut each strip into 1/8-inch pieces. The tiny cubes should be square in appearance.

Use the tiny cubes just as you would breadcrumbs. First coat the item to be fried with Binding Mixture, page 16, then roll in tiny cubes. If you find the cubes don't evenly or completely cover the object to be fried, no problem. Simply dip a cube in the Binding Mixture and place it in any empty spot. It's helpful to use tweezers, because the cubes are small.

If the appetizers you are making are shaped into balls, make them slightly smaller than you ordinarily would because rolling them in the tiny cubes will increase their size. Large appetizers are not attractive or elegant.

MERMAIDS' MARBLES

Shrimp of any size may be used in this recipe because they are pureed.

1 lb. fresh shrimp
pinch of white pepper
1 large egg white
1 tsp. salt

pinch of sugar
1 tbs. vegetable oil
oil for frying or boiling water

Shell, devein and rinse shrimp. Dry with paper towels. In two or three batches, blend shrimp, pepper, egg white, salt, sugar and 1 tablespoon vegetable oil together in blender or food processor until pureed. Heat oil in wok or skillet to 275°F., or heat water to same temperature. Each should be a depth of about 3 inches. Place about 2 heaping tablespoons of shrimp mixture in the palm of your hand. Close fingers and squeeze, leaving thumb and first finger slightly open. The mixture will come through this opening in the shape of a ball. It should be about 1 inch in diameter. Using your other hand and an oiled spoon, scoop the shaped mixture off your hand and drop it into the hot oil or hot water. Cook for about 1 minute. They cook quickly and are done as soon as they turn pink. Drain on paper towels and serve immediately.

SHRIMP TOAST

(48 Pieces)

This recipe is appreciated for its deliciousness and because it can be prepared in advance. The frying time is only a few seconds.

24 medium shrimp
2 tbs. Binding Mixture, page 16
1 tsp. salt
pinch **each** of onion powder,
   pepper and sugar

12 slices fresh bread (make 48 bread
   rounds, using 1-1/2-inch
   round cutter)
2 cups breadcrumbs
oil for frying

Shell shrimp. Cut in half lengthwise and remove vein. Wash and soak in cool water 10 minutes. Dry with paper towels. Combine Binding Mixture with seasonings. Brush bread rounds with mixture. Place 1 shrimp neatly and flat on top of each bread round. Reverse the whole piece and press into a bowl full of bread crumbs. Heat oil in wok to 350°F. Fry rounds, shrimp-side down, for 5 seconds. Turn and fry until bread rounds are a light golden brown. Remove and drain on paper towels with bottoms up until serving time.

FRIED CAULIFLOWER

(32 Pieces)

Broccoli can be prepared this way, too. However, the cooking times are not the same. The final products are very different in appearance and taste, but both are delicious.

1 head cauliflower
Nine-Three-One Batter, page 35
1 tbs. each salt and oil, in one quart water
1 pinch pepper powder
oil for deep-frying

Wash and cut cauliflower into small flowerets. Prepare batter. Allow one cup batter for each 12 flowerets. Bring water with salt and oil to a boil. Simmer the cauliflower for three minutes. Drain (do not rinse) and sprinkle with pinch of pepper. Just before frying, dip each piece in batter. Fry in wok in oil at 325°F. Cauliflower can be prepared in advance. Just before serving re-fry at 350°F. for ten seconds. The actual absorption of oil is not much, but three cups will be needed for a depth of two to three inches.

FRIED PARSLEY

This recipe is used in fancy restaurants for garnishing. Don't prepare it in too large a quantity. It is so delicious that when you prepare Nine-Three-One Batter for any recipe in this book, you should make an extra cup of batter and treat yourself to this recipe.

1 bunch parsley   Nine-Three-One Batter, page 35
1 pinch salt

In advance, pick out 8 to 10 nice long stems of parsley with lots of leaves on them. Rinse, drain and allow to dry thoroughly. Dip in the batter and let excess drip back into bowl rather thoroughly before frying. Heat oil in wok to 350°F. Fry parsley until golden brown then cut into two-inch lengths. Lightly sprinkle with salt to serve—a nibbling appetizer. Because the parsley is fried in the whole length of its stalk, you need more batter to cover it properly. Therefore, if you're frying a variety of foods, it is better to fry the parsley first.

SHAW'S APPETIZER

(About 12 Rolls)

Sir Alfred Hitchcock, the movie genius, once teased the slim vegetarian, Bernard Shaw: "Now I SEE there is famine in the world!" Shaw, the sarcastic writer, looked at the stout Alfred and replied: "Now I KNOW why!"

This appetizer is based upon those two talented persons' conversation.

1 head Napa cabbage
1 carrot
1 stalk celery
1 cup vinegar

1 tsp. salt
1 tsp. sugar
1 tbs. sesame oil
1 bunch cilantro

Remove the leaves from the cabbage carefully to avoid breaking. Wash well. Cut the root part into 2-1/2-inch lengths, then cut into thin strips. Cut carrot and celery into strips to match. Combine seasonings in a large mixing bowl. Add whole cabbage leaves and vegetable strips. Let stand for an hour. Remove the leaves and drain. Add cilantro to remaining vegetables. Place a small amount of marinated vegetables on each cabbage leaf. Fold part of leaf over filling, then fold sides in and roll as a package.

FRIED WON TON

Pre-cook the stuffing so it will be ready when you fry the won ton. Fry until it is golden brown. Because it is cooked with added flour, less moisture will be released. This keeps the final product from becoming soggy.

1 lb. ground beef
2 tbs. soy sauce
3 tbs. all-purpose flour
pinch of pepper and sugar
pinch of onion powder
1 lb. won ton wrapping (85 sheets)

Using no oil, cook the beef on low heat, breaking up any lumps, until it is done. (You are actually conducting a test to see how much fat your butcher has included with the ground beef!) Sprinkle the meat with flour, a little at a time, until the meat turns into a dough-like ball. Test the seasoning, keeping slightly to the generous side because the wrapping is not seasoned. Fill and fold the won ton as illustrated. For better results and to cut your last-minute rush, you may fry stuffed won ton hours

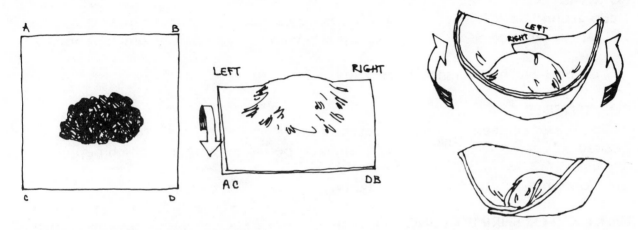

ahead and fry again briefly just before serving. Heat oil in wok to 350ºF. and fry won ton just until they start to change color. Remove from oil and drain well. When ready to serve, merely lower the already-fried won ton into hot oil as if you were going to par-boil them. This introduces a Chinese technique: double-frying.

VARIATIONS OF FILLINGS
FOR WON TON

PORK FILLING

1 cup ground pork 1-1/2 tbs. soy sauce 1 tsp. sugar
1/2 tsp. sesame oil 1/2 tsp. dry wine 1 pinch pepper

Combine all ingredients thoroughly.

CHICKEN FILLING

1 cup minced chicken 1 tbs. soy sauce 1/4 tsp. salt
1/2 tsp. sugar 1/4 tsp. chopped fresh ginger 1 pinch pepper

Combine all ingredients thoroughly.

FISH, CRAB OR SHRIMP FILLING

1 cup sea fish, crab or shrimp 1 tsp. salt 1/4 tsp. white pepper
1/2 of an egg white 1 tbs. cornstarch 1 tbs. cooking oil

Combine all ingredients thoroughly.

VEGETARIAN FILLING
FOR DEEP FRIED WON TON

(96 Pieces)

Make these small and delicate. They will be a hit at any party.

1/2 cup onion strips
1/2 cup green pepper strips
1/2 cup celery strips
1/2 cup cooked carrot, cut in tiny pieces
2 tbs. soy sauce
2 tsp. salt
2 tbs. cooking oil
2 tbs. cornstarch
won ton wrappers

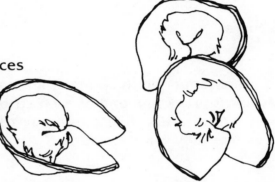

Partially cook onion, green pepper and celery, separately, in small amount of oil. Mix vegetables, seasonings, oil and cornstarch together. Place 1 teaspoon filling in center of each won ton wrapper. Fold as illustrated on page 69. Heat oil in wok to 350ºF. Fry won ton until golden brown. Serve with one of the Dipping Sauces on pages 68 and 69.

DEEP FRIED WON TON TIES

(2 per Wrapper)

These crunchy little ties are quick to make and always popular at parties. Serve with Sweet and Sour Sauce, page 68.

won ton wrappers
oil for frying

Cut won ton wrappers in half. Make a lengthwise slit about 1 inch long in the middle of each strip. Tuck one end of each strip back through the slit. Carefully pull and shape neatly into a tie. Heat oil in wok to 350°F. Fry ties until golden brown. Don't over brown or they will taste burned.

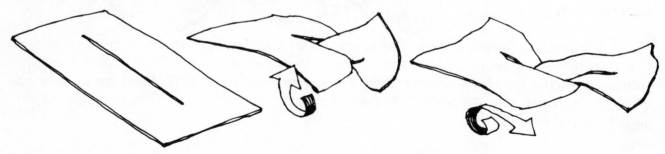

EGG ROLLS

This is not a true egg roll, but a modification of won ton.

won ton wrappers
Filling, choice of 1 from page 88
1 beaten egg
1 tbs. all-purpose flour
1 tbs. cornstarch
1/4 tsp. salt
2 tbs. water
oil for frying

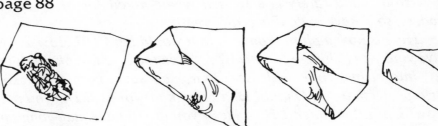

Prepare filling. Combine egg, flour, cornstarch, salt and water. With one corner of wrapper pointing toward you, place 1 rounded teaspoon of filling just above corner. Fold corner up over filling and tuck it under filling. Roll once and fold left and right corners. Roll closed. Seal tip with a small amount of egg mixture. Let dry a minute or two. Dip whole roll into egg mixture. Heat oil in wok to 325°F. Fry rolls until golden brown.

Recipe by Telephone The Chinese Way

The Chinese style of asking for a recipe and the reply are very different from the American way. A few minutes of verbal instruction is enough for most recipes. Small details are not furnished unless requested. Established methods and logic are expected to be understood, and rarely is a written recipe asked for or given. This will not work for my readers, so, I have to do things differently.

Here is how a phone conversation would be: "Hi! How are you? . . . I'm fine. Did you have your rice (Chinese for meal)? . . . Me too . . . Lobokau? It is simple. Cut the turnip . . . yes, into strips, cook with rice flour, add some cornstarch, some oil, sausage and dried shrimp, steam it . . . Oh, no! Don't thank me for this! Did you play mah-jong yesterday? . . . Wow! Up 'till midnight! How lucky you are to have mah-jong partners. Here I cannot even smell the mah-jong, it is all covered with mold! (Chinese for being left for a long time.) . . . Okay, bye, bye. I will call you next Sunday (for weekend rates). Bye."

Some telephone company stockholders must be very unhappy with the Chinese!

Although I scripted this conversation, it is true to life. Giving a recipe takes only minutes between Chinese. Now, will you agree that I had to plan this book in a different way?

OPEN-FACED SANDWICHES FOR APPETIZERS

This section may be extended to thousands of varieties if we want. We can use different kinds of bread, shapes and endless combinations of meats and spreads. Only one sample is used here for you.

Atop a round piece of fresh bread, place a dab of mayonnaise, then a slice of boiled egg, a slice of canned beet and finally tiny bits of parsley. Use the right size of cutter, so the bread is slightly larger than the egg, and the beet slice is smaller than the yolk. A dab of mayonnaise is used to hold the yolk on the bread and to add taste. Keep the mayonnaise away from the edges of the bread for a clean appearance. Fresh bread is better than crackers because of its softness and it can be cut into any size or shape.

SHAPING OPEN-FACED SANDWICHES

A neatly shaped appetizer will be eye-catching. You will be proud to serve them. How about a short phrase in fluent Mandarin when you serve? Say, "Ching, ching," with your right palm facing up as you approach the person you are serving. Everyone will understand what you are expressing—Please, please—especially if you say it with a friendly smile!

If you don't know this method, handling soft and sticky food is not fun at all. Read the instructions carefully. You will be surprised at how easy it is to form a neat hemisphere for appetizers using bread rounds as a base.

Use a small spoon, the shape should be flat and round as used for feeding babies. Hold the bread round in one hand. Use the other hand to spoon the filling or whatever is called for by the recipe. Take one spoonful of food. DO NOT pile it on the bread round. Instead, hold the spoon with the handle pointing downward, at a position just higher than the bread round. SCRAPE the filling mixture from the spoon by using the bread round. Hold your spoon steady, turning the bread round about a quarter-turn. Keep turning and scraping (even if there is no more food in the spoon) until the top hemisphere is neat. Done properly, it is very fast and your fingers will remain clean.

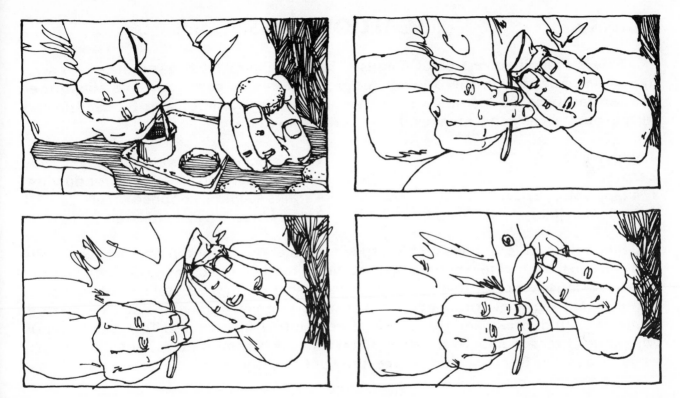

SCALLION PUFFS

This is a modified version of Chinese "Tsung U Ping." Its size is reduced for serving as an appetizer. In the original recipe, pork lard is called for. I've substituted chicken fat, because it's much easier to obtain. Vegetable oil can be used in this recipe, but the chicken fat makes the puffs richer in taste.

4 egg yolks
2 tsp. salt
1/4 tsp. white pepper
1 tsp. lemon juice

1 cup chicken fat or vegetable oil
1 tsp. cornstarch (plus some for dusting)
4 stalks scallion, chopped
8 slices bread, lightly toasted

Blend the first four items on high speed in a blender or food processor. Gradually add chicken fat, a half teaspoon at a time, then 1 tablespoon cornstarch, until mixture turns the consistency of thick mayonnaise. Dust the chopped scallion all over with about 2 teaspoons of cornstarch. Fold scallion into thick mayonnaise-like mixture. Trim crusts from bread and discard. Cut bread into 1-inch circles. Top bread rounds with about 1 teaspoon of thick mixture. It will be slightly mounded. Keeping the puffs as far as possible from the heat source, broil until lightly browned.

Chinese Food As A Crystal Ball

I don't know how expert pollsters can explain their silly predictions during elections! Using Chinese food as a crystal ball, I am happy with the past trend in my record, ten out of ten times proven true.

John LLoyd, C.B.E., British Consul General in San Francisco, liked Chinese food and was promoted to Ambassador in 1970.

James Murray, C.M.G., exchanged his bacon and eggs for Chinese congee and was transferred from San Francisco to UN as Minister of the British Mission there.

Herb Caen, who inspired me to write the recipe Fish Ping Pong, in this cookbook, was selected as one of the ten most influential persons in San Francisco.

Earl Goldman was willing to publish **The Wok.** *Having a self-contained printing company on large acreage in Concord, California, he rolled the book off the presses and it became one of the widest published cookbooks.*

Ronald Reagan was enjoying the Chinese food hosted by the British Consul, pocketing the menu before the dinner was over. He is now President of the USA!

Gary Lee ate Chinese food all of his life; he's a happy teacher and cookbook author. Well . . . as mentioned earlier, the chances are ten out of ten—it pays to like Chinese food!

SPECIALTIES FROM OLD CHINA

There are about forty some Chinese cooking methods which are not so easy to translate into English without a lot of explanation. Here are some practical tricks which you might like to learn and use.

LOOOING is a typical old Chinese cooking method. It is slow-cooking in a strongly seasoned broth which is called Looo. Any kind of tough meat will turn out soft and tender after a proper length of time in the Looo. It is really a very practical cooking method once you can have the Looo stored in your freezer.

QUENCHING is like the blacksmith heating a piece of iron red-hot then immersing it in cold water (some chemicals are added) to turn the iron harder (tempering). When this method is used for food, it will absorb the seasoning from the Quenching Mixture and the texture will also be changed.

SMOKING in Chinese cooking is done only to add flavor. The food must first be cooked.

HOME CURING was a necessity in the days before refrigeration.

APPETIZERS FROM THE POT OF LOOO

(6 Cups)

This cooking trick is simple, infallible and versatile. First, food is partially cooked, then it is immersed in dark or white Looo to complete the cooking and insure good flavor. But, what is Looo? It basically is a method of storing, in liquid form, subtle spices and food essences. Looo can be kept indefinitely but must be boiled each time before using. The longer Looo has been used the better the taste as each food being Loooed leaves a little of its flavor behind. Looo that has been used many times will gel when chilled. The broth used in making Looo can be chicken, beef, pork or a combination. It should be unseasoned and well strained. See pages 168 and 170 for more about making and straining broth.

DARK LOOO

1 qt. homemade broth	6 tbs. sugar	1 tsp. cinnamon
2 cups dark soy sauce	1 star anise seed	

Combine all ingredients and bring to a boil. Use as directed in appetizer recipes on next page. After you use the Looo, strain and freeze. Before heating again, scrape away hardened fat on top. Each time you use the Looo, add small amounts of soy sauce, sugar and spices to compensate for what was lost.

APPETIZERS

Chicken Wings — Cut through two joints making 3 pieces (see page 36). Discard tips. Parboil in water to cover for 5 minutes. Drain. Immerse in boiling Looo. Remove from heat. Cover with lid and let stand for 2 hours. Wings will continue cooking in the hot Looo. Lift wings from Looo and serve cold — a nice finger food.

Chicken Drumsticks — Buy the smallest drumsticks you can. Parboil 5 minutes. Drain and Looo as directed above. Serve cold.

Giblets — Leave whole. Prepare and Looo as directed above. Slice liver and gizzards after they are cold. Give hearts a fancy touch. From the tips, make a cross-cut half way down. It will open like a tiny flower. Place a tiny bit of parsley in the center. Serve cold.

This recipe makes enough Looo for at least 100 chicken wings, drumsticks, giblets or a combination of all.

ROSY DUCK

(40 Cubes)

The seasoned broth used in this recipe is actually a kind of white Looo. Read about Looo on page 104.

1 duck, 4 to 5 lbs.
4 to 5 tbs. curing salt (see page 119)
3 qts. unseasoned chicken broth (see pages 168 and 170)

2 tbs. salt
1 tsp. Flower pepper (or nutmeg)
1 clove star anise
sesame oil

Use 1 tablespoon of curing salt per pound of duck. Rub duck inside and out with salt. Place in plastic bag. Force all air out of bag. Seal tightly. Refrigerate for 3 days, turning bag every 24 hours. Rub and squeeze the duck from the outside with each turning. After 3 days, rinse duck thoroughly. In a Dutch oven, or other large pan, cover duck with broth. Add salt, Flower pepper and star anise. Bring to a boil. Reduce heat, cover and simmer for 15 minutes. Turn off heat. Leave pan on stove, covered. When duck is luke warm, remove it from the pan. With paper towels, wipe off fat from duck. Rub entire surface with sesame oil. Cover and chill until firm. For appetizers, cut into small cubes and serve on toothpicks.

(25 Pieces per Pound) # HOMEMADE HAM

For those who like ham, this is better and cheaper than buying sliced ham.

1 fresh pork butt, with skin and bones
1-1/2 tbs. curing salt per lb. of pork
4 to 5 qts. unseasoned chicken broth (see
  pages 168 and 170)

2 tbs. salt
1 tsp. Flower pepper
1 clove star anise

Rub pork butt all over with curing salt. Place in plastic bag. Force air out of bag. Seal tightly. Refrigerate for 3 days, turning every 24 hours. Rub and squeeze the pork butt from the outside with each turning. After 3 days, rinse the pork thoroughly. In a large pan, cover pork with 3 quarts of the broth. Add salt, Flower pepper and star anise. (This is White Looo.) Bring to a boil. Reduce heat, cover and simmer about 1 hour or until skin is **very** tender. While the meat is still warm, you can effortlessly remove the bones. Wipe away excess fat. (Strain Looo and freeze it.) Place the boneless butt in a large bowl, skin side down and pour remaining unseasoned broth over meat to cover. Place a plate on top and apply a weight, about 10 pounds, to firm it. Chill 10 hours. Cut into domino-size pieces. Malt vinegar with grated ginger added can be used for dipping.

WEDGES OF LOOO

(20 Wedges)

Looo is very delicious for an appetizer, but how to serve it? I have found a way to serve it in wedges and the base holding it will never likely be misunderstood as edible. Or those who do not have well-developed Looo which will gel (see page 104), use Cheating Looo.

CHEATING LOOO:
2 cups Swanson's chicken broth **or**
2 cups Campbell's beef broth
1 envelope unflavored gelatin
2 oranges, cut in half

Place broth (chicken for white Looo or beef for dark Looo) in refrigerator for several hours. Punch a hole in the bottom of can and place over bowl. Punch another hole in top of can. Broth will run out the bottom and the grease floating on top will be trapped in can. Soften gelatin in broth. Heat to dissolve gelatin. Squeeze oranges and save shells. Scrape as much white fiber from shells as possible. Fill shells with well-established Looo or Cheating Looo. Chill until firm. Cut into wedges and serve. Presto—a pretty and tasty appetizer.

QUENCHING

Quenching is a technique often used in Chinese cooking. The quenching procedure is very simple: deep-fry the food then plunge it into a cold mixture immediately, like a blacksmith immerses the red-hot iron in cold water. The seasoning in the mixture will penetrate and replace the food's natural moisture, and the sudden change in temperature will firm the food's texture. Blacksmiths use cold water or a chemical solution. We cooks use mixtures of different kinds of seasonings.

This technique has certain advantages. The quenched eggplants in the recipe for Empress Fan, page 110, will be thoroughly seasoned without a long period of cooking. The quenched smelt in the Smoked Fish recipe on page 116, will have very soft bones yet the meat will still be firm.

The quenching mixture should be prepared for each individual food accordingly.

EMPRESS FAN

The first time I tried this Eggplant Sandwich was in Brazil, 1955. I liked it and changed the cutting method plus added a typical Chinese cooking technique of Quenching, and named it Empress Fan. Egg-size eggplants are sometimes obtainable in Chinatown, San Francisco, but not very often. If this variety cannot be found, the name of this recipe is not completely correct, and we have to cheat a little bit.

Quenching Mixture

   1 clove garlic, finely mashed
   3 tbs. light soy sauce
   1 tbs. sugar
   3 tbs. water (or more to taste)
   1 tsp. sesame oil
   1 lb. small or large eggplant
   1 loaf sourdough bread, thingly sliced
   oil for deep-frying

   Prepare quenching mixture by combining garlic, soy sauce, sugar and water. Add

110   Specialties from Old China   Continued

sesame oil just before using. Cut the thin, foot-long eggplants into slices, then cut the bread rounds to an appropriate size to match. If large, round eggplant is to be used, first slice, then cut eggplant slices and bread with a cookie-round cutter. Fry the eggplant slices immediately after cutting or they will turn dark. Fry in small batches in oil at 325°F. until they turn soft, about one minute. You should be able to feel it with your heat-resistant fingers—chopsticks. Remove from oil and immediately quench them in the quenching mixture. If you set up everything before frying, you should be able to fry the second batch right after you finish the first. When the second batch is almost ready for quenching, take the first batch from the quenching mixture, and so forth until you finish the job. Serve cold on top of bread rounds. The finished egg-plants can be kept for a week in the refrigerator, so you can prepare them in advance. Leftovers are good for lunchbox sandwiches.

TO SMOKE IN A WOK

Ever since I was a very young boy, I enjoyed reading my favorite magazine, **Popular Mechanics,** the Chinese edition, of course. I was then and still am impressed by all the Westerners' ingenuity in solving problems in their daily lives—except in home cooking. It seems that Chinese cooking methods are often simpler and less expensive than Westerners'! I am sure there are few Chinese in the USA who have a food smoker, yet Chinese do have smoked dishes by using a wok!

Food is fully cooked and ready to serve; all we need is to add some smoke flavor—a matter of only several minutes.

In a wok, combine one tablespoon sugar and one tablespoon dry tea. Use chopsticks or whatever to form a rack like the symbol "#." On this rack, lay the cooked food. Heat the wok on medium heat until the smoke starts, cover with a lid and turn to medium-low heat. Don't smoke too much or the taste will be too strong.

Different kinds of tea will produce different flavors. You can also use bamboo leaves, needles of pine trees or saw dust. For simplicity, tea and sugar are the handy match.

SMOKED EGGS

The method used here is revised from **The Wok,** which I wrote in 1970. Thirteen years amount to a lot of days, and I constantly try to polish my rusty skills.

For appetizers, buy the smallest eggs. You don't need to pierce them with a needle as I watched one demonstrator do. Place a plate in a pan, lay eggs on the plate and cover with water for 15 minutes. Bring the water to 160°F. and stop! Rinse with cold water, then raise the heat again. This time stop at 170°F. Remove eggs from pan and cool completely with tap water. To shell, we'd better ignore any gadget on the market and follow the simple and sure way of the Latin Americans: Crack the egg shells on a hard countertop lightly, on the lengthwise side. Roll egg back and forth with your palm with just enough pressure to break the shells. After eggs are shelled, bring the Looo (see page 104) to a boil. Cool to 150°F. Immerse eggs in this overnight. The next day, take out the eggs and proceed to smoke them in a wok (see page 114). To serve, cut into halves with a cheese cutter or wire. Yolks are expected to still be runny. Sprinkle a few drops of Looo on the yolk for better taste.

SMOKED FISH

Different kinds of fish can be used, but smelt, or white bait are the best choice because of their diminutive size.

Quenching Mixture:
   1/3 cup soy sauce
   2/3 cup water
   1 tbs. sugar
   1 tsp. Five Spice Powder

1 lb. smelt or white bait
1/2 tsp. fresh ginger juice
1/4 tsp. salt
1 tbs. soy sauce
1 tbs. loose tea
1/2 tsp. sugar

Combine all ingredients for Quenching Mixture in a bowl. Set aside. Using a sharp knife or kitchen shears, cut the underside of the fish open. Rinse out and pat dry with paper towels. Season interior of fish with ginger juice, salt and soy sauce. Place in colander, over bowl, and refrigerate overnight. Pat dry with paper towels next day. Heat oil in wok to 350°F. Fry fish 5 to 6 at a time, until they brown and begin to curl. When done, plunge into Quenching Mixture. When second batch of fish is done, remove first batch from Quenching Mixture and set aside to drain. Place second batch in mixture and continue process until all fish are used. When all fish are cooked, clean wok. In bottom of wok, put tea and 1/2 teaspoon sugar. Place a rack in wok. Heat until mixture smokes. In small batches, smoke fish covered, about 5 minutes, or until they reach desired degree of smoky flavor. (See To Smoke In A Wok, page 114.)

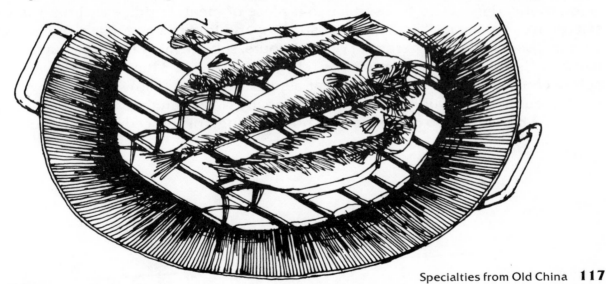

HOME CURING

Home curing is using curing salt or pure salt to draw out the natural moisture from the meats and allowing the taste of salt to penetrate them.

Weigh the meat and figure out the equivalent of 4% of that weight. This is the amount of curing salt to be used for that piece of meat. Sprinkle and rub the curing salt all over the meat. Place it in a plastic bag and fold the bag. Place the bag in the warmest spot of the refrigerator. Every 24 hours, rub the meat from the outside of the bag (Lazy Lee!)—and put it back in the refrigerator. About 3 days later it will be ready. Before cooking the meat, give the meat a quick rinse and follow the cooking instructions of each recipe. During the curing period, by classic method, some heavy weight should be placed on top of the meat. In home curing, this procedure may be omitted.

CURING SALT

Saltpeter is sold without prescription and will be used in the following recipes. If you don't like to use it, disregard curing salt and use pure table salt instead. Why is saltpeter used? It firms the meat, adds more flavor, prevents the spoiling of meat during the curing period, and turns meats the color of ham, which somehow we all like. To use or not use it, please ask your doctor. However, label the curing salt if you do use it.

In a blender, add 1 cup of rock salt and blend. Add 1 teaspoon saltpeter and blend again into fine grains.

The proportion is about 48:1, less than 2% of saltpeter vs. 98% rock salt. As we need less than 5% of curing salt for meats, by weight, the actual saltpeter is less than 1% of the meat's weight. One whole duck, chicken or a 2-pound portion will serve more than 10 persons. Therefore, each person's serving has less than 0.01% saltpeter.

The Growth Of Chinese Cuisine

The Chinese language is complex. Yet it is much simpler than it used to be. Thousands of ancient words (characters) are kept in libraries and now used for reference only. Modern forms of abbreviations plus the traditional speedwriting, which almost every person knows, allow the Chinese to save a great deal of time in handwriting. For example,   (ten thousand) is now   .

Conversely, Chinese cooking offers many new dishes as new methods and equipment are introduced. From remote areas which were once inaccessible come shrimp, seedless melons and other exotic ingredients. They are grown on farms and shipped to consumers in the cities. Modern technology makes this possible. New equipment and tools also make way for new cooking methods.

In 1970 when I wrote THE WOK*, I mentioned thirty cooking methods used by Chinese chefs. Now, there are roughly forty different ones. Using a combination of the same methods in different order, such as "fry then steam" or "steam then fry," creates entirely different dishes and the combinations are almost endless.

Overall, I think modernization is a good trend. The Chinese can now spend less time writing (Character Typing Machines are for printers only) and devote more time to the crea-

*Copyright 1970, Nitty Gritty Cookbooks; Revised 1982. In 28th printing.

Continued

tion of new dishes. Of course, new dishes will not solve worldwide problems, but tasty dishes are more palatable than A bombs or X bombs.

There are only about 2000 words used by the Chinese to cover every field while an equal number of terms are **added** to the English dictionary every year. You might wonder how the Chinese people can manage that!

It is simple: by using a combination of words. Locomotives, automobiles and bicycles all have wheels so they are grouped as "car," then distinguished from each other by adding the source of power—fire-car, gas-car and foot-pedaled-car. This Chinese method of identifying things allows every Chinese to understand a new term immediately. However, many combinations of words will make no sense to readers if translated literally: open-heart (happy), close-heart (concerned), dotting-heart pronounced as Dim Sum which is described in the Light Snacks section of my book.

fire-car   gas-car   foot-pedaled-car

DIM SUM

Dim Sum can best be translated as light snacks or tidbits. It has the following characeristics: It is not a regular meal. Its portions are small. Most dim sum are morsels of meat-stuffed or sweet dumplings. They can be steamed, deep-fried or baked and are often served with hot and spicy dips. More substantial dim sum includes noodle dishes and chow mein.

Establishments that serve only dim sum are called tea houses in Canton. Elsewhere they are identified by the particular type of dim sum they specialize in— The Golden Dragon Noodle Store, The Silver Dragon Steamed Bun Store, The Old Dragon Won Ton Store, etc. As you may have guessed, dragons are very popular in China! Here is an interesting aside for readers. A blue dragon is a good dragon. A red dragon is responsible for making the air hot in the summertime. His hot breath makes the temperature rise. The black dragon is associated with rain and fog. Chinese people sometimes refer to a person who does everything wrong as a black dragon and oolong tea is sometimes called black dragon. Peter Sellers' detective movies are popular in China. Inspector Cluseau is referred to as Detective Oolong. An apt description, don't you agree?

In China, dim sum fall into one of three categories: morning, afternoon and late night. These divisions are not faithfully followed outside of China. Dim sum are always accompanied by tea or beef or chicken broth served in tea cups.

It would be easier to know a thousand Chinese recipes by heart (because one recipe leads to another) than it would to know the countless varieties and variations of dim sum served in all the Chinese provinces.

I would like to take on this task, but I already have to work hard. Uncle takes most of my earnings, because he spends a lot! Besides, this project would take many years and the eldest brother in our family will not postpone his appointment with me. His name is Saint Peter! So, instead of giving you thousands of recipes, I give you my favorite ones.

BASIC RULES FOR SEASONING DIM SUM

Because Dim Sum is not a conventional dish, its seasonings are different. This page contains some basic rules to guide you.

Both soy sauce and salt are salty tasting. The soy sauce is in liquid form and tends to add color and flavor, but it also tends to overbrown food when fried. Salt is dry so it does not add moisture as it flavors the food during the cooking process. For example, shrimp and fish are delicate, so salt is preferred. Its dryness keeps the food from becoming soggy.

With this simple rule in mind, you can decide which to use. When soy sauce is used, a pinch of sugar will harmonize the taste and pepper will always be helpful in giving a pleasant aroma—just a pinch! Ginger is good with fish, garlic and onions will enrich the flavor of meat and wine can replace water in many recipes. Never add wine to seafood before cooking, it will become soggy.

In general, for each pound of meat use LESS than 1 teaspoon of salt or 2 tablespoons of soy sauce.

Last rule in cooking: Season on the light side and adjust to your taste.

STEAMING TIPS

A LITTLE BACKGROUND

The lack of large quantities of easily obtained cooking fuels has caused the Chinese to become very economical in their cooking methods. The sloping sides of the wok tend to seal in the heat of the clay fire pot on which it is traditionally used. Little of the heat potential is lost in comparison to the "western-style" flat bottom pan. Also, the high heat or temperature used in Chinese-frying saves fuel as well as preserving flavor and food value.

However, there are some foods that require a longer, gentler and more even cooking process, such as steaming. Fortunately, the very things that make the wok good for Chinese-frying help make it an efficient steaming apparatus. Since most Chinese families already owned a wok, it was only natural to adopt it for this task by inventing stackable bamboo steaming trays. This unique combination of wok pan and bamboo steaming trays has many valuable features. The main one is the ability to cook many separate things at once with the same amount of fuel, whether one tray or six is used. As the steam rises, it passes through the various trays, cooking each piece of food evenly on all sides. Thus, very little steam heat or energy is lost and the fuel requirement is kept low.

STEAMING DIM SUM IN CHINESE TEA HOUSES

It is not unusual for a Chinese tea house to have a specially built stove with gas-fired wok pans up to 40 inches in diameter. These pans accept stacks of steaming trays eight to ten high and up to 36 inches around! Large hoods are then lowered down onto the woks and hundreds of dim sum dumplings can be steamed at once.

Trays of various kinds of dim sum snacks, three or four to a plate, are brought to the table by a waiter or waitress and the patron may choose as many or as few as he wishes. At the end of the meal, the empty plates are counted and charges are made accordingly. Sharp mustard, vinegar and hot sauces of various kinds are served as condiments.

STEAMERS IN REVIEW

Bamboo Steaming Trays — These circular, stackable, interlocking trays are hand-made from layer upon layer of bamboo laminated together. This heavy, layered construction insulates the trays and even keeps food warm until serving time. They are

Continued

quite inexpensive and are usually available where woks are sold. Their main value is the ability to cook many separate things at once with the same amount of fuel. As the steam rises it passes through the loosely woven bottoms of the various trays, cooking each piece of food on all sides. Try cooking broccoli, cauliflower or any favorite vegetable, or even pork chops in a Chinese steamer for unusual and pleasing results. Fish also lend themselves to steaming because they cook quickly and must be treated gently.

The use of the steaming trays is not limited to Chinese food. A "western-style" dinner of steamed ribs, broccoli and potatoes is just one example of a meal that can be prepared on a stack of bamboo trays with very little effort. And, although they were designed to go with a wok, the bamboo steaming trays will work in a large pan or skillet.

Steaming Racks—Most woks come with some kind of a simple steaming rack, such as two wooden sticks, each with a notch cut in the middle so they fit together to form a cross. It is placed over water in the wok, then any heat-proof plate or dish, holding the food to be steamed, can be set on the rack. The wok cover retains the steam. Sometimes these small racks packaged with a wok are made of stainless steel and shaped like a tic-tac-toe sign or a wagon wheel. They fit into the wok like the cross-shaped wooden racks and are used the same.

Steaming Without A Steamer—A Chinese bamboo steamer does the best job because it absorbs moisture and there is less condensation on the food. However, such a steamer is not always available and everybody may not even have a wok! I'll give you a tip: adapt a pan, or better still, an electric skillet, as a steamer.

Place a cookie rack in the pan, fill with boiling water to one inch or **just below** the rack, then place the food on the rack. Heat at medium-high on the stove or at 250ºF. in the electric skillet. Always wipe the inside of the lid dry before starting to steam. Watch by **listening** to the noise of the water left inside. If you think the water has all escaped, fill again with boiling water. Keep the lid off only as long as absolutely necessary. In most cases, one filling will be sufficient. A lid that matches the pan is adequate, but don't try to have the lid fit too tightly or you'll turn the process into pressure cooking. We cannot cook an omelet without an egg, but we certainly can steam without a steamer.

(20 Dumplings)   # SHRIMP DUMPLINGS

1 cup Dung Mein* or cornstarch
1 cup boiling water
1 tbs. lard or chicken fat
1/2 tsp. salt

1 cup shrimp, shelled, deveined and
   chopped
1/4 cup bacon fat, raw and chopped
1/4 cup bamboo shoots, finely chopped
1/2 tsp. salt and pinch of white pepper

To make dough, mix first 4 ingredients in a saucepan with a wooden spoon. Cook until thick. Cool. Combine remaining ingredients. Use a piece of marble slab or smooth formica about 8 inches square. For each bun, place a 1-inch ball of dough on

Make pleats
on one side
of rolled dough
and fill.

the oil-rubbed slab or formica board. Flatten the ball with an oil-rubbed cleaver, press firmly as far as it will go. Use the cutting edge of the cleaver to lift the dough. It should be thin and round in shape. Stuff dough with filling. Fold it neatly as illustrated. Steam in wok over high heat (be sure to line the steamer with oiled cheesecloth first) for 10 minutes and serve. Properly done, the dough is transparent and not sticky and gummy.

*Dung Mein is the starch from wheat flour. If not available, use cornstarch.

Bring edges together

Seal edges

and steam

PORK SHAOMAI
(STEAMED DUMPLINGS)

(85 Dumplings)

Traditionally, preparing the wrapping for Shaomai is the most difficult part because it calls for skill and a special rolling pin. Let's cheat a little by using won ton wrappers. Keep dumplings covered until ready to steam so they don't dry out.

1 lb. boneless pork butt	1 tsp. salt
1 tbs. light soy sauce	1 tsp. sugar
1 tsp. dry vermouth	1 pinch white pepper
1 tbs. sesame oil	round won ton wrappers

Cut pork into pea sized pieces. Add seasonings and stir vigorously until well mixed. Place about 1 teaspoon of stuffing in the middle of won ton wrapper. Gather up wrapper to enclose filling, letting the dough pleat naturally. Squeeze to seal. Pat sides to firm, and tap bottom to flatten. Place on plate. Steam in wok on high heat for six minutes. (See page 128 for more about steaming.)

If round wrappers aren't available, use square ones. The unevenness of the corners is actually attractive.

BEEF AND RICE SHAOMAI

(85 Dumplings)

This is a northern Chinese Dim Sum. Because it is inexpensive to make, it is one variety which has been popular as a breakfast snack.

1 cup cooked rice
1 cup ground beef
1 tbs. sesame oil
1 tbs. soy sauce

1 tsp. salt
1 pinch each white pepper and sugar
round won ton wrappers

The rice should be cooked so it is dry. Combine with beef and seasonings. Follow directions given for Pork Shaomai, Page 136, for assembling. Place on plate and steam in wok on high heat for five minutes.

Fold corners in and up making pleats

Pat sides and squeeze

Tap bottom

(80 Buns) CLASSIC DOUGH FOR STEAMED BUNS

It will take about 10 hours for this dough to be ready. You might not want to try it, but it is included for your information and reference. Bicarbonate ammonia can be purchased from a pharmacy. Its pungent odor disappears in cooking.

8 cups all-purpose flour
2 tbs. baking powder
1 tsp. bicarbonate ammonia
2/3 cup water

1-1/2 cups sugar
1/2 cake yeast
1/2 tsp. baking soda
2/3 cup milk

Mix all ingredients until smooth. Leave dough in a covered bowl at room temperature for fermentation, about 8 to 10 hours (winter or summer). During this time, knead thoroughly at least twice. Prepare filling during the waiting period. See pages 140 and 142 for how to shape and steam buns.

(20 Buns) # INSTANT DOUGH FOR STEAMED BUNS

This is much more practical in our busy daily lives. Only 15 minutes and you'll have the dough ready for steaming!

2 cups self-rising flour
1/3 cup sugar
1/4 cup lukewarm milk
1-1/2 tsp. baking powder
3 tbs.lukewarm water
1 tbs. lard

Mix all ingredients together into a smooth dough. Cover the dough and let rest for 15 minutes. Have the stuffing ready in advance. (See pages 140 and 142 for how to shape and steam buns.)

TO SHAPE THE BUNS FOR STEAMING

There is no established rule as to what size the bun should be. As a lunch, you might prefer it large like a hamburger bun. As a Dim Sum, a smaller bun is more elegant, and no one needs to share one bun with someone else.

One ounce (about 2 tablespoons) of dough will be about right for each bun. Shape the dough in the palm of your hand. Press hard with your palm and flatten the ball into a circle, making the edges thinner than the center. Because the dough is soft, you do not need a rolling pin to enlarge the size. Simply pinch the edges slightly; after you stuff, fold each of the pinches to the center.

Cooked buns can be frozen in plastic bags. When you re-heat them, first thaw in the bag, then place on a rack and steam for five minutes.

I discovered that by placing the buns upside-down when re-heating, the piece of lining paper can be easily removed without tearing the bottom of the bun.

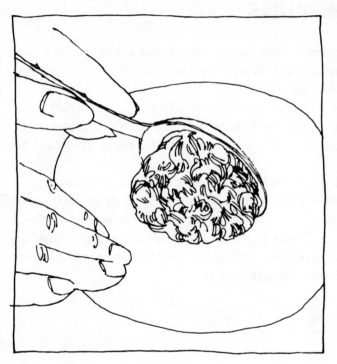

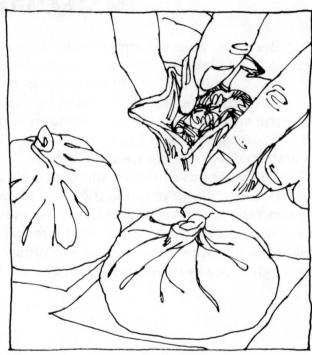

TO STEAM THE BUNS (PAO)

Because the local temperature influences fermentation and our kitchens are not equipped as laboratories, some adjustments must be made. One method is to steam the buns immediately after folding and shaping.

The other method is to let the buns sit for another 15 minutes on a covered tray. But the steamer should be reasonably tight and the water just under a vigorous boil. It takes roughly 8 to 12 minutes for each batch, depending upon the heat source and number of buns in the steamer.

The water used for steaming should be pre-calculated to the right amount, or it will not be enough to finish the job. This will force you to refill with water before completing the steaming process. Approximately 3 to 4 inches between the water surface and the bottom of the buns will be required. Place a piece of waxed paper or cooking parchment under the uncooked buns to prevent sticking to the steamer. Leave enough space between the buns, as each bun will get larger.

CHICKEN AND CHESTNUT BUNS

The variations of stuffing for steamed buns are too many to be listed. This is a good one—too good for commercial use—so you can hardly find it in restaurants.

6 oz. (3/4 cup) freshly shelled chestnuts
1-1/2 tbs. cornstarch
1-1/2 tbs. oyster sauce
a pinch sugar (nuts are sweet)
2 tbs. chicken fat

1/2 tsp. sesame oil
1 tbs. light soy sauce
1/2 cup water or unseasoned broth
1 cup finely-diced chicken meat
Instant Dough For Buns, page 139

Steam the shelled chestnuts for 30 minutes. Mash them slightly but not into a paste. Mix together remaining ingredients except the chicken and chestnuts. Heat to boiling. Cool and add the chicken and chestnuts. Chill before filling buns. Prepare dough as directed. See pages 140 and 142 for shaping and steaming instructions.

(3 to 4 Cups)   # BARBECUED PORK

In order to make Pork Buns, we have to start by making our own barbecued pork or purchasing it from a Chinese restaurant.

2 lbs. boneless pork butt
2 tbs. soy bean paste
2 tbs. dry vermouth

3 tbs. honey
2 tbs. hoi-sing sauce*
1 pinch Five Spice Powder

Cut the pork into 1/4 x1-1/2-inch strips. Combine remaining ingredients in a bowl. Marinate meat in mixture for an hour. Remove from marinade. Place on rack in shallow pan and roast in oven at 325°F. for about 25 minutes. Check and adjust the heat. Slightly burned tips will not cause a problem, instead they will improve the flavor. Excessively burned tips may be trimmed later.

*If you cannot find the bean paste and hoi-sing sauce, use: 2 tablespoons light soy sauce and 2 tablespoons tomato ketchup instead.

BARBECUED PORK BUNS

(20 Buns)

The main thing is to cut the pork into nail size pieces. This adds more taste and smoothness to the stuffing for the buns.

1 shallot, chopped
1 small yellow onion, chopped
1 tbs. oil
2 tbs. cornstarch
1 tsp. sugar

1 tbs. sesame oil
1 cup water
2 tbs. oyster sauce
2 cups Barbecued Pork, page 144
Instant Dough For Buns, page 139

Cook the shallot and onion in oil over medium heat until tender. Add remaining ingredients, except pork, and continue cooking until sauce thickens. Cool and mix in the pork pieces. Chill the batch thoroughly before using. Prepare dough as directed. See pages 140 and 142 for shaping and steaming instructions.

(26 Meatballs) **MEATBALLS OF COLORED PEARLS**

This recipe was originally from the Hupeh province where the revolution sparkled and last Emperor Sientung crumbled. Rice used in this recipe can be tinted with food color or by using the juice from beets and spinach. Very colorful, indeed!

1 lb. ground pork
1 tbs. soy sauce
1 pinch sugar and pepper

1 cup short grain rice, soaked overnight
1 tsp. beet juice
1 tbs. spinach juice

Mix the pork, soy sauce, sugar and pepper together. Shape mixture into 3/4-inch balls. Divide the pre-soaked rice into three parts. Tint one-third red in the beet juice and another one-third green in the spinach juice, leave one-third white. Roll the balls in each batch of rice to coat them evenly. Steam in wok on high heat for 15 minutes on an oiled cheesecloth to avoid condensation and sticking in the steamer.

(Makes 12)

RED SAILS IN THE SUNSET

If you know this lovely song, I wish: "Home Safely To You!"

6 small zucchini
4 ozs. ground beef
1-1/2 tsp. soy sauce

1 pinch sugar and pepper
1 tsp. cornstarch
12 thin slices of carrot, diagonally cut

Cut the small end off of each zucchini leaving about 2-1/2 to 3 inches of the larger end. (Reserve the small end for another use.) Holding a zucchini in one hand, shape the cut end into a point with a vegetable peeler, turning zucchini as you shape. Now, cut in half lengthwise. Hollow out centers, leaving about a 1/4-inch rim. Now, you have 12 tiny boats. Flatten bottoms if necessary, using the peeler. Cut carrot slices into triangles to resemble sails. Place in ice water until needed. Combine beef, soy sauce, sugar, pepper and cornstarch. Shape into a pattie. Steam boats, bottom side up, and pattie separately, 5 minutes. Rinse boats in cold water and dry with paper towels. Break steamed pattie into blender container and blend a few seconds to a fine-grain paste. Spoon filling into boats and add carrot sails. Now, "Anchors Away!"

CABBAGE ROLLS

(Makes 8)

This recipe is an entree for a fancy and formal Chinese dinner because of its lightness and elegant taste. Therefore, it also fits for serving as a Dim Sum.

1 whole Chinese cabbage
1 tbs. cornstarch
3/4 cup diced chicken breast
1/4 cup diced bamboo shoots

1 tbs. green peas
2 tsp. light soy sauce
1 tsp. sesame oil
1 pinch each salt and white pepper

Cut out and remove the core from the cabbage. Remove 8 of the best leaves. Parboil until soft enough for easy rolling, but not too soft. Drain and pat them dry with paper towels. Sprinkle evenly with cornstarch on both sides of the leaves. Combine remaining ingredients. Divide into 8 balls. Place one ball on each of 8 leaves. Roll into little envelopes. Steam rolls in a wok on high heat for 15 minutes. Drain and serve.

GINGER AND SCALLION NOODLES

(6 Servings)

A good combination does not need too many items. If we make a soup with chicken, duck, pork, beef, ham, and also many vegetables, it would be tasty but with no character.

1 lb. fresh egg noodles
5 tbs. oil
4 stalks scallion, chopped

2 tbs. finely chopped fresh ginger
1/2 cup Chinese oyster sauce

The amount will be enough for four servings as a lunch Dim Sum. Cook the noodles in plenty of boiling water with a tablespoonful of oil, but no salt. Have another kettle of boiling water on hand. When the noodles are done, about 2 minutes, drain; rinse thoroughly with the boiling water and drain again. Meanwhile, heat 4 tablespoons of oil in a wok until smoking. Arrange the noodles in a serving platter with chopped ginger and scallions on top. Pour the hot oil over to "burn" the ginger and scallions. Add oyster sauce and mix thoroughly. Soy sauce should be available for individual tastes.

CHOW MEIN—HONG KONG STYLE

This name is familiar to most readers—a Chinese noodle dish. The method used here is not the same as many Chinese-American restaurants offer.

Noodle preparation: Should be cooked in advance, but rinsed with cold water, followed by a coating of heated oil so noodles won't stick together. Chill noodles covered. This improves the texture. Color is important to this dish. To shorten the cooking time and obtain the desired color, use a very small amount of soy sauce, sprinkle on the cooked noodles and mix well. On low heat in an uncovered pan or wok, heat until the batch of noodles is hot, crisp and brown. Turn and do the same on the other side.

Seasoning is not required, since a topping of meat, vegetables with seasonings and sauce will be added. See next page for some examples of toppings.

One pound of noodles makes six light snack servings.

TOPPINGS FOR CHOW MEIN—HONG KONG STYLE

Toppings for Chow Mein are actually dishes, prepared in the most popular way of the Chinese—fried.

In applying the toppings, there are certain unwritten rules. For instance, there is no Fish Chow Mein, but there is Shrimp Chow Mein.

Meat can be beef, pork, chicken or shrimp and ham, in slices or strips.

Vegetables are limited to Chinese cabbage, celery, onion, scallions, broccoli or varieties that are crunchy (e.g., spinach is never used).

Tomato is matched with beef and onion, plus ketchup—a perfect combination for Americans.

Seasoning consists of soy sauce and a pinch of sugar and pepper. For a gourmet touch, some mashed garlic may be used for stronger flavor.

Sauce in the style described in Mountainous Noodles, page 154, should be generous—to cover the whole portion of noodles, but only as much as can be absorbed.

The cooking method is rather conventional. Heat the wok, add some oil, then the ingredients. After one minute, add some broth or water. One minute later add cornstarch mixture to thicken the sauce, then pour on top of the noodles.

MOUNTAINOUS NOODLES

This was my favorite dish when I was young and I still enjoy it!

1 lb. thin fresh noodles
cooking oil
4 tbs. sesame oil
1/4 cup crunchy peanut butter
1 clove garlic, mashed

1/4 cup light soy sauce
1 tbs. Tabasco sauce
1/2 cup malt vinegar
1 tbs. Worcestershire sauce

Cook noodles in plenty of boiling water, adding 1 tablespoon cooking oil for each 2 quarts of water. When noodles are done, drain, rinse with tap water and drain well. Heat 2 tablespoons of the sesame oil and mix into drained noodles. Chill at least 1 hour. Blend remaining sesame oil and peanut butter into a paste. Add garlic, soy sauce, Tabasco, vinegar and Worcestershire sauce. Stir until well blended. Mound chilled noodles neatly on a platter and serve the sauce in a separate bowl. Allow guests to combine noodles and sauce to suit their own tastes.

MOUNTAINOUS NOODLES AS A CENTERPIECE

This is an attractive dish for a buffet luncheon. Mountainous Noodles are surrounded by garnishes and the sauce is served separately in a small bowl.

Mountainous Noodles, page 154
vegetable oil
1 egg, beaten
1 bunch cliantro, leaves only

1 cup bean sprouts
1/2 cup cooked, shredded chicken breast
1/2 cup cooked ham strips
8 red radish roses

Prepare noodles and sauce as directed in recipe. Chill until needed. Place a large skillet over medium-high heat. Sprinkle a few drops of oil into skillet. Use a paper towel to distribute oil evenly. Pour beaten egg into skillet. Cook without stirring until done. Remove from skillet and cut into 1/3 x 2-inch strips. Pile noodles neatly on a platter. Surround with garnishes, starting from the outer edge of the platter in the following order: cilantro leaves, bean sprouts, egg strips, shredded chicken and ham strips. Garnish with radish roses. Serve sauce in separate bowl.

SWEETNESS IN CHINESE COOKING

Sweetness is very important in Chinese cooking. Sugar is mostly used for its inexpensiveness. Honey is used for roasting, as it tends not to burn as easily as sugar. Use honey on a pot roast to produce a thicker sauce—shiny and tasty! Sugar made from wheat gemmae is used for that famous fried chicken to keep the skin crisp. Artifical sugar is used for pickles as it draws less natural moisture from vegetables than real sugar.

In many Chinese dialects, to describe the deliciousness of a dish, the word FRESH is used; in Cantonese the word SWEET is used. Both are correct. Any dish (salty dishes served for meals) must contain a slight sweetness, almost unnoticeable, to bring out a deliciously blended taste. MSG has this effect. We can use sugar, in the right amount, if we don't like to ingest the chemical product. MSG will not help an entirely sweet dish, which needs salt to bring out the flavor. So, nothing is actually very new under the sun. Our grandmas already knew how to add a pinch of salt to sweet pies and vice versa. Chinese add a pinch of sugar to salty dishes for that same effect.

Before I married my wife, Hedy, she called me SWEETHEART. The first 15 years she changed it to HONEY; the second 15 years she addressed me as SUGAR. The next 15 years, she probably will term me CYCLAMATE!

STEAMED CAKE

(9- or 10-inch Cake)

The Chinese must bow to Westerners when it comes to cakes and desserts. However, I have created this little steamed cake which tastes good after Dim Sum.

2 tbs. lard
5 eggs, separated
2 cups sugar

2 cups all-purpose flour
1/2 cup raisins or currants
6 red maraschino cherries

Cut a piece of waxed paper large enough to line the bottom and sides of a 9- or 10-inch springform cake pan. Grease the paper with the lard. Beat the egg whites until foamy. Gradually add sugar and continue beating until stiff, but not dry. Beat yolks slightly. Gently cut into egg whites alternately with flour. Stir in raisins. Cut cherries into thin rings. Distribute evenly over the bottom of the prepared pan. Pour batter into pan. Steam in a wok for 15 minutes on high heat. (See page 128 for more about steaming.) When slightly cooled, cut into wedges and serve with bottom up.

PINEAPPLE TOAST

When pineapple was introduced to the Chinese, they had never seen a fruit with such a funny shape, so they named it Phoenix Pear, after the legendary bird which nobody knew. This name is still used in Taiwan.

4 cups crushed pineapple, preferably fresh
1-1/2 cups sugar
1/4 cup butter or margarine
1/4 cup cornstarch

4 egg yolks
1 loaf, good quality white bread
oil for frying
margarine for frying

Combine pineapple, sugar and butter in saucepan over medium heat. Stir until sugar dissolves and butter melts. Remove from heat and cool. Stir in cornstarch. Cook again until thickened. Cool. Stir in egg yolks and chill. For each sandwich, spread pineapple mixture about 1/4 inch thick on a slice of bread. Top with second slice. Heat a tablespoon each of oil and margarine in a skillet over medium heat. Brown sandwiches on both sides. Trim crusts and cut each sandwich into bite-size pieces.

NUT PUFFS

(32 Puffs)

In its original form this recipe called for red-bean paste, which is difficult for readers to get. Therefore, I modified it calling only for those ingredients which can be found locally.

10 egg whites
1/4 cup all-purpose flour
1/4 cup cornstarch
1/2 cup chopped peanuts

2 tbs. peanut butter for binding
oil for frying
powdered sugar

Beat the egg whites until they barely hold soft peaks. Gently fold in the flour and cornstarch. Combine the nuts and peanut butter. Shape into marble-sized pieces, dip into the egg white mixture and fry in wok in oil at 325°F. until golden brown. To serve, sprinkle with powdered sugar.

GINGER MILK

This is Chinese magic! Thickening hot milk with fresh ginger juice. Add a little sugar and presto—a tasty drink.

fresh ginger root
1 qt. whole milk
sugar

Finely grate fresh ginger on a ginger or nutmeg grater, then squeeze the juice out. Measure 1 teaspoon ginger juice into each of 4 cups.* Heat milk slowly in a heavy saucepan over low heat until volume is reduced to 2-3/4 cups. Pour about 2/3 cup hot milk into each cup over the ginger juice. Leave undisturbed for a minute or two. When the milk looks slightly thickened, it is ready to serve. Sweeten to taste. What magic!

*Most fresh ginger comes from mature roots. It is juicer, has more acidity and more flavor than young roots, and 1 teaspoon of its juice will be enough to thicken each serving of milk. If ginger is not mature, more juice will be needed. Experiment with the first cup and adjust to that amount in the remaining servings.

SOFT MILK CUSTARD

(2 Servings)

The primary concern when preparing this popular Dim Sum is the temperature at which it is steamed. It must be kept low.

1 cup evaporated milk
1/2 cup water
1 large egg white
sugar to taste

1/4 tsp. almond extract
pinch salt

Combine ingredients and beat thoroughly. Add slightly more sugar than you think you'll need. The taste of the custard will be less sweet after it is cooked. Go relax for 10 minutes, then pour custard mixture into individual serving bowls. Place the steaming rack in the wok. Add hot water to just below the rack. (The temperature of the water should be about 200°F.) Place custards on rack. Cover and steam over medium heat about 20 minutes or until set.

Double or triple this sweet treat, if desired.

CUSTARD TARTS

Pastry:
- 1 cup all-purpose flour
- 1 cup cake flour
- 1/4 cup **each** chilled lard and butter
- 1/4 cup sugar
- 1 large egg
- 1/4 cup ice water

Filling:
- 1/2 cup milk
- 3/4 cup cream
- 3/4 cup sugar
- 3 egg yolks
- 2 whole eggs
- 1 tsp. vanilla

Combine flours in large mixing bowl. Cut lard and butter into flour. Stir in sugar. Beat egg and water together. Add to flour mixture, tossing lightly with a fork until mixture forms a dough. Knead 5 times on a lightly floured board. Wrap in plastic and chill 15 miniutes. In large mixing bowl combine filling ingredients. Beat just until blended. Divide chilled dough into 24 pieces. Press pieces of dough into muffin tins. Each little shell should have about 1-inch high sides. Prick shells lightly all over. Partially bake in 400°F. oven for 8 minutes. Remove and reduce temperature to 325°F. Pour a heaping tablespoonful of filling into each shell. Return to oven and bake 10 to 15 minutes or until custard is just set. Makes 24 tarts.

Using part lard in the pastry gives it just the right flavor and texture.

(50 Pieces) ## SWEET HALF MOONS

Sweet food for the Chinese is reserved for special occasions. By the Chinese moon calendar, every month's 15th day is Full Moon. If you serve this recipe accordingly, you should only have it on the 7th and 23rd days of each month. It is a No Sugar Diet—Chinese version!

1/4 cup sesame seed, lightly browned
1/4 cup crunchy peanut butter
1/2 cup sugar

1/4 cup shredded coconut
round won ton wrappers
oil for frying

Sesame seed can be black or white. Brown in a dry wok gently until they release their aroma. To make filling, combine sesame seed, peanut butter, sugar and coconut. Fill the round wrappers with one heaping teaspoonful of filling. Wet the edges and fold. Pinch them firmly together. Fry in wok in oil at 300ºF. until lightly browned. Do not over-fry as a small amount of moisture from the filling is desirable. Drain on rack. Cool before serving. Store in a cookie jar.

WON TON IN SOUP

Won Ton Soup is a dinner course, while Won Ton in Soup is a Dim Sum.

1 lb. ground pork
4 oz. shrimp, chopped
1 tsp. soy sauce
1 tbs. sesame oil
1 tsp. salt

1 pinch white pepper
1 lb. thin won ton wrapping
2 qts. seasoned broth
1 stalk scallion, chopped

Combine pork, shrimp, soy sauce, sesame oil, salt and pepper. Place 1 teaspoon filling in center of each won ton skin. Fold as illustrated on page 87. Heat broth to about 195°F. in pan. Heat water to boiling in another large pan. Add the won ton to the boiling water, simmer for one minute; add one cup of cold water to stop the simmering. Keep at the same medium heat and when water comes to a boil again, simmer for 30 seconds. Using a slotted spoon, remove the won ton and place into serving bowls. Fill each bowl with broth to cover; sprinkle chopped scallion on top and serve. Have pepper, salt and soy sauce available for individaul tastes.

(1 Quart)   SOUP FOR DIM SUM, CHICKEN FLAVOR

Each cook has a different method for preparing a simple chicken consomme. Here is the simplest.

1 chicken cut up (not including giblets)
salt and white pepper to taste

Use enough boiling water to cover cut-up chicken parts. Cook on high heat for one minute. Turn the heat down, just below the simmering point and cook without a cover. Leave it undisturned for one hour. First remove the chicken parts, then strain broth (see page 170). You'll get what you expected: chicken broth as clear as water! Season to your taste with salt and white pepper.

When chicken is cooked too long, the broth will be muddy, especially when cooked on high heat; and the taste will not be much improved. Simmering without a cover will assure the right temperature yet the chicken meat will still be tender. You can use the cooked chicken for some other recipe—chicken salad or chicken a la king.

Soup for dim sum is served in teacups to be sipped—spoons are not used.

SOUP FOR DIM SUM, BEEF FLAVOR

(1 Quart)

There is not a single soup served in a Chinese restaurant or at home with only one ingredient. This soup is a kind of drink that goes with Dim Sum, served in a small teacup with no soup spoon. It has only one ingredient, salt is not counted. For all these characteristic differences from ordinary soups, its original name is literally, in English, Beef Tea. It must be clear, without grease, and strong in flavor.

1 lb lean ground beef
1 qt. water

1 tsp. salt or to taste
1 pinch white pepper

No matter what price you pay for ground beef, it always has beef fat mixed with the lean meat and only lean meat is needed for this recipe! Chill a mixing bowl in the freezer for 15 minutes. Place the freshly ground beef in the bowl. Stir to loosen the meat. After about 30 seconds, the beef fat will stick, like a coating, to the bowl. Gently lift out the meat, leaving the fat behind. In another bowl, combine meat, water, salt and pepper. Chill in refrigerator for 2 hours. Then bring mixture to a simmer over medium heat. Cook, uncovered, for 2 minutes. Strain and serve.

Try the above method when you want to remove the extra fat from ground meat.

TO DEGREASE BROTH

There are several ways to degrease broth. Using paper towels is messy and a substantial amount of broth is wasted. Using the chilling method is good, but you have to wait. The magic mop sold on the market is interesting, but cleaning the mop is tedious. My favorite is the **Double Strainer Method.** You need a pair of strainers, one coarse and the other very fine. Place the coarse one on top of the fine one. Pour broth through both strainers. The top one will trap large pieces, while the fine one will refine the straining job without too much possibility of clogging. Watch the dripping when it nears the end and don't let any sediment come through. Remove strainers and rinse fine one in hot water. Use it to skim floating grease from the broth in a sweeping motion. Wash both strainers in hot soapy water. To make the broth crystal clear, add 1 beaten egg and simmer for 10 minutes. The egg will jell the impurities which will then be very easy to strain from the broth through the fine strainer.

TEA AND THE CHINESE

It was noted by the Chinese thousands of years ago that the seven most needed items to start a day were firewood, rice, oil, salt, soy sauce, vinegar and tea. A Chinese meal without tea is unthinkable, and this book without a few words about tea would be incomplete because it is the beverage traditionally served with both appetizers and dim sum.

In order to make a good cup of tea, tap water must be boiled for several minutes to rid it of added chemicals. Cool it for one minute or until the temperature is about 200°F. before brewing your tea. This will make the tea "sweeter" because of the natural reaction of the tannic acid.

The brewing time and strength of tea varies according to the kind of tea used and personal taste. One practice is to brew a pot of rather strong tea and have another pot of hot, boiled water on hand so each person can adjust the strength to individual taste.

The high content of tannic acid in tea helps digestion, therefore tea is always served during a Chinese meal. The glass of ice water that Westerners prefer is considered by old Chinese as a troublemaker for the stomach. Tea is perferably served hot or at least warm so its aroma can be enjoyed.

For brewing tea, porcelain teapots are the most popular, but the very best are earthenware teapots from the province of Checkiang. They are also the most expensive. One teapot can cost as much as one thousand dollars. They were invented long ago by the monks who washed the local muds in barrels with plenty of water and then let them set. The water was poured off along with the first layer of mud, which is the finest material for making teapots. Before a teapot made by Checkiang potters is used, it should be thoroughly washed and well rinsed. Then its inside is never washed again. It should only be rinsed with hot water. The tea cures the pot and it continues to mellow and improve with age.

Many ingenious designs for teapots have been created. I have one without an opening in the top. There is a hole at the bottom which is actually a tube extending to the height of the spout. You can turn the teapot over and fill it with brewed tea, turn it right side up and the tea will not run out from the bottom as you pour it through the spout. Another interesting design is the pot with a spout resembling a dragon, which is also a whistle. When you pour the tea the dragon whistles.

There is a superstition that two teapots placed on one table should not be facing each other or quarrels will occur.

If you like jasmine tea which is one of the most popular, you can tell the quality of the tea by the number of flower buds found mixed in with the tea leaves. The best jasmine teas have no flower buds, but you might pay five times more for them.

Many old traditions involve tea. To offer a cup of tea is considered as a respectful gesture when the bride is introduced to her husband's family members after the wedding ceremony. Those who have the honor of receiving such a cup of tea present a sealed red envelope containing money to the newlyweds as a wish for their happiness.

The tea serving ceremony requires the host to pour the first cup for each guest. A younger guest then helps in further pouring, starting from the right and going to his left, serving his own last.

When someone is pouring tea for you, tap your fingers twice in front of your cup. This is a polite way of saying "thank you."

TO YOUR HEALTH

Sir Winston Churchill excelled in his command of the English language and his word power is famous and highly regarded. My English seems as though I had taken a Winston English course in the United States from the ad man who composed the famous slogan:

"Winston tastes good, like a cigarette should!"

Many letters poured in which pointed out the grammatical error. The company defended with, "You want good grammar or good taste?"

How nice! Now I can stop worrying about my poor English! So I say to you:

To your health!
Gary's appetizers taste good
Like all appetizers should!
After all, do you want good grammar
Or good Chinese appetizers?

I hope you enjoy my recipes.
Gary Lee

INDEX

METRIC CONVERSION CHART

Liquid or Dry Measuring Cup (based on an 8 ounce cup)

1/4 cup = 60 ml
1/3 cup = 80 ml
1/2 cup = 125 ml
3/4 cup = 190 ml
1 cup = 250 ml
2 cups = 500 ml

Liquid or Dry Measuring Cup (based on a 10 ounce cup)

1/4 cup = 80 ml
1/3 cup = 100 ml
1/2 cup = 150 ml
3/4 cup = 230 ml
1 cup = 300 ml
2 cups = 600 ml

Liquid or Dry Teaspoon and Tablespoon

1/4 tsp. = 1.5 ml
1/2 tsp. = 3 ml
1 tsp. = 5 ml
3 tsp. = 1 tbs. = 15 ml

Temperatures

°F		°C
200	=	100
250	=	120
275	=	140
300	=	150
325	=	160
350	=	180
375	=	190
400	=	200
425	=	220
450	=	230
475	=	240
500	=	260
550	=	280

Pan Sizes (1 inch = 25 mm)

8-inch pan (round or square) = 200 mm x 200 mm
9-inch pan (round or square) = 225 mm x 225 mm
9 x 5 x 3-inch loaf pan = 225 mm x 125 mm x 75 mm
1/4 inch thickness = 5 mm
1/8 inch thickness = 2.5 mm

Pressure Cooker

100 Kpa = 15 pounds per square inch
70 Kpa = 10 pounds per square inch
35 Kpa = 5 pounds per square inch

Mass

1 ounce = 30 g
4 ounces = 1/4 pound = 125 g
8 ounces = 1/2 pound = 250 g
16 ounces = 1 pound = 500 g
2 pounds = 1 kg

Key   (America uses an 8 ounce cup - Britain uses a 10 ounce cup)

ml = milliliter
l = liter
g = gram
K = Kilo (one thousand)
mm = millimeter
m = milli (a thousandth)
°F = degrees Fahrenheit

°C = degrees Celsius
tsp. = teaspoon
tbs. = tablespoon
Kpa = (pounds pressure per square inch)
    This configuration is used for pressure cookers only.

Metric equivalents are rounded to conform to existing metric measuring utensils.